Praise for *Elephant in the Classroom*

"With a true teacher's soul and a leader's insight and channeling the acumen of the National Board for Professional Teaching Standards, Maxey describes the vital elements for teacher success, including what each element looks like in action, the research behind each element, and what the implications in teaching are for each one. His writing is clean and does not waste the practitioner's time, as every sentence leads somewhere substantive. *Elephant in the Classroom* is a wonderful, 'true north,' compass heading for both new and veteran teachers, leaders, and policymakers trying to perceive the inter-connected mosaic that is teaching. For anyone just starting, anyone outside of teaching, or for seasoned veterans, this is a lucid deconstruction of a very complex endeavor."

— **Rick Wormeli**, national board-certified teacher, author, educational consultant

"If we are to better educate our kids, we need first to better educate their educators. This book examines and analyzes what goes into the vast complexities of a successful teaching profession. Andrew Maxey deals with what educators should expect from their profession, as well as what the profession expects from educators. It is a guide through a system most Americans have experienced with varied results and lasting opinions. This book strives to bring clarity, through research and experience, as a guide to better educating our educators for the sake of educating our kids."

—**Tom Whitby**, educational author, blogger, #Edchat founder, and social media influencer

Elephant in
the Classroom

Elephant in the Classroom

Tracing the Complexity of Teaching by Exploring 13 Competencies and Practices

Andrew Maxey

ROWMAN & LITTLEFIELD
Lanham • Boulder • New York • London

Published by Rowman & Littlefield
An imprint of The Rowman & Littlefield Publishing Group, Inc.
4501 Forbes Boulevard, Suite 200, Lanham, Maryland 20706
www.rowman.com

86-90 Paul Street, London EC2A 4NE, United Kingdom

British Library Cataloguing in Publication Information Available

Library of Congress Cataloging-in-Publication Data

Names: Maxey, Andrew, author.
Title: Elephant in the classroom : tracing the complexity of teaching by exploring 13 competencies and practices / Andrew Maxey.
Other titles: Tracing the complexity of teaching by exploring thirteen competencies and practices
Description: Lanham, Maryland : Rowman & Littlefield, [2022] | Includes bibliographical references. | Summary: "Elephant in the Classroom is an exploration of the vast complexity of teaching as it is described by research and experienced by teachers"—Provided by publisher.
Identifiers: LCCN 2021035471 (print) | LCCN 2021035472 (ebook) | ISBN 9781475862393 (Cloth : acid-free paper) | ISBN 9781475862409 (Paperback : acid-free paper) | ISBN 9781475862416 (ePub)
Subjects: LCSH: Teaching. | Teaching—Research.
Classification: LCC LB1025.3 .M3445 2022 (print) | LCC LB1025.3 (ebook) | DDC 370.7—dc23
LC record available at https://lccn.loc.gov/2021035471
LC ebook record available at https://lccn.loc.gov/2021035472

∞™ The paper used in this publication meets the minimum requirements of American National Standard for Information Sciences—Permanence of Paper for Printed Library Materials, ANSI/NISO Z39.48-1992.

To the countless men and women who have done profession-level work as teachers even though they were denied the rights and privileges that are provided for professionals; and to the current and yet unborn students who each deserve to be taught by professional, accomplished teachers.

Contents

Foreword

The longstanding ignorance and downplaying of the complexity of teaching within mainstream public opinion came to a screeching halt with the COVID-19 pandemic. Parents quickly learned that managing a child's learning—let alone multiple children's learning—takes real skill. From coast-to-coast, workplace water cooler chit chat turned to workplace zoom moaning about the impossibilities of simultaneously maintaining student engagement, guiding academic development, tending to social-emotional needs, and managing educational technology. "How on earth do teachers do this?" asked nearly every parent in the country.

Amidst the tragedy of the pandemic is the silver lining of the public's renewed appreciation for teaching as the complex and demanding profession that it is. No longer could it be said that anybody can teach. The unveiling of the true, challenging nature of this work opens a window of opportunity to change the trajectory for how we as a society invest in this profession that makes all others possible. Before, as long as the public could conveniently under-appreciate the complexity of teaching, public officials could direct limited taxpayer resources toward other priorities, maintaining salary levels and workplace conditions that are not reflective of other complex professions like medicine, law, and engineering. Now, teaching cannot so easily be brushed aside as a job any warm body can handle. Efforts to address ongoing teacher shortages cannot ignore the fact that positions must be filled by professionals—professionals who have been trained and demonstrated mastery of a complex set of skills, knowledge, and dispositions.

However, changing this trajectory of how the public views, treats, and invests in the teaching profession requires that those closest to the work—including teachers, leaders, scholars, and advocates—can speak coherently to the complexities of teaching. The field of education must help put into words the experience of overwhelm that so many parents felt as they were forced to attempt teaching themselves.

The Elephant in the Classroom provides the framework to articulate the complexity of teaching—so that educators themselves can make sense of all that it means to teach and then elevate the public's burgeoning understanding of teaching's complexities. At this moment in history when public receptivity is at its highest, it is incumbent upon educators and those who support educators to carry the messages set forth in this book, in order to replace outdated and harmful mischaracterizations of the profession with a more complete and accurate portrayal of what it looks like to teach well.

By picking up this book you have taken the first step in re-shaping what it means to be a teacher today. You are in the company of many other teachers, leaders, teacher-leaders, and advocates who have laid a strong foundation. Teachers of the year, National Board Certified Teachers, fellows with organizations like Teach Plus, and union and association leaders have led countless initiatives, local and national, to elevate the teaching profession. This book is a useful tool for taking this work to professionalize teaching to the next level. Now is the time—so turn the page and let's get to work!

Ellen Sherratt, PhD
Board Chair, Teacher Salary Project

Acknowledgments

This book has its origins in an interaction in a graduate school discussion thread. I made the claim that teaching is impossibly complex. Dr. Angela Benson first reminded me that a scholar provides evidence and support for claims. But it was her second comment that got this ball rolling—*If there's a problem, do something about it.* A few months later, my quest to describe the boundaries of teaching as I had experienced, witnessed, and studied it became the seed that germinated into a research study that formed the heart of this book. Heartfelt thanks to Dr. Vivian Wright for nurturing this work. It was she who first asked why I should not focus my research here; she who supported my insistence on keeping that research at the breadth it needed to be; she who first suggested that this work should not stop with a dissertation. It was she who first called me a *scholar*. Her encouragement and masterful persistence provided the fuel to keep working when it would have been much more restful to stop.

It seems inconceivable to consider that anyone with experience as a teacher for any amount of time will be at all surprised by the competencies and practices described in this book. The details of the experience of teaching obviously vary but only insofar as the details of the lived experience of *any* profession do. So it seems important to acknowledge the hundreds of teachers I have seen in action up close. My own teachers across more than twenty-four years of formal schooling, my teammates through nine years of teaching in three states, and everyone I have worked with closely as a school and district administrator. This map of teaching is drawn from the research but it is also an accurate depiction of what I have seen in practice. Thanks especially to each of the teachers who participated in formal interviews, gave permission for the use of quotes, and provided the models for the examples provided.

The influence of a few researchers and practitioners will probably be hard to miss in the following chapters. While thousands of scholars have been and are studying a mind-boggling array of the parts of teaching and learning, I am especially indebted to a few who have spent years and decades studying *all* of teaching. In particular, the work of Linda Darling-Hammonds and Marc Tucker on teaching as a profession *and what exactly that means* suggested to me that there is a place for taking a snapshot of the entire forest that is teaching in order to complement our faithful study of all the leaves and branches in it.

Each implication and conclusion volunteered in this book is based in part or entirely on the evidence I have personally observed in practice. While each non-example I have observed has been instructive in its own way to my learning and growth as a professional teacher, a few examples of unassuming, matter-of-fact models of excellence have stood tall as signposts on the road for me. While they are too many to mention here, I send special thanks to Mr. John Devore who provided the best example of effective leadership I have seen in my twenty-plus years in public education. More than one recommendation that follows was modeled by him as a natural part of his practice as principal. Whether he would label it this way himself or not, he modeled, without fail, a commitment to treating teachers like professionals.

Finally, profound thanks to the four amazing women with whom I live. It is incredible to be partnered with a woman so deeply committed to service and to the empowerment of others. Lori, a hụrụ m gị n'anya! The three fierce young adolescents who keep my heart full also motivate me to remain committed to making every contribution I can to the improvement of education both for their sake and for the sake of the generation they may one day parent.

Introduction

We Need a Map

Most individuals born before the proliferation of smartphones and who traveled outside their hometown share a memory. The memory of using a paper map or atlas. Today the travel atlases Rand McNally still produces have to compete with the GPS-enabled turn-by-turn directions your phone issues for the right to guide travelers. But at one time, one had to be very adventurous to travel any significant distance without at least consulting a map.

The mapping of real things is not limited to roadways. Landmasses, ocean currents, political boundaries, watersheds, public transportation lines, and geological topographies are just a tiny sample of the things that have been mapped. Maps are often created through the close observation or survey of thousands of points of data. Some maps provide a great deal of detail throughout the document; while each detail is a valuable part, it is the cohesion, the unification of all those disparate details that give a map its value.

Education in general, and teaching in particular, has been and continues to be the subject of an incredibly vast body of research. Researchers and practitioners alike strive endlessly to develop a deeper understanding of the field.

Entire bodies of research literature are dedicated to relatively small and focused areas such as specific areas of practice (i.e., phonics instruction vs whole language instruction) and entire journals are dedicated to specific subsets of practice (i.e., *Research in Middle Level Education* and *Journal of Physical Education, Recreation and Dance*). Conferences, newsletters, blogs, and practitioner publications are *everywhere*. In spite of this great wealth of research and knowledge, public education does not have a map that unifies what we know about teaching. There simply is not a description that encompasses all of the process and act of teaching.

That is not to say that teaching is a mystery. The professionals doing the job know it. The educators charged with leadership are well familiar with it.

Researchers spend decades studying it carefully. The problem this book seeks to address is not that we don't know enough about teaching but that we don't have a frame for the whole of what we know. We don't have a map.

This presents several problems. First, it allows a *lot* of misconceptions about teaching by folks outside education—including some who have the authority to make decisions *about* schools and teaching. But this lack of a map of the whole of teaching is also problematic for people who *are* familiar with it—school- and district-level administrators. They are familiar with all the parts of teaching but struggle to hold that entire complexity in their heads when they make decisions that impact teachers and their work directly. These—and other factors—contribute to a most troubling trend: the de-professionalization of teaching.

Richard Ingersoll, researcher and education professor, argues that teaching meets all the criteria for being a profession. For example, credential and licensing requirements, induction programs, and professional development expectations and support. He (and others) also argue, however, that teaching is being radically *de*-professionalized. Teachers are expected to produce professional-level work but they are denied the benefits other professionals enjoy particularly in regard to autonomy, voice, compensation, and prestige or occupational social standing.

The great complexity of teaching marks it as a true profession. But the tendency to miss or forget that complexity blocks and diminishes efforts to raise teaching to full professional status and to maintain progress in that regard.

Maps are only as valuable as they are accurate. Producing an accurate map requires an examination of the area it depicts. Any map of teaching must likewise be based on the evidence and not on personal perspective or opinion. The map of teaching offered in this book is based on an extensive review of the available information.

The first phase was a systematic review of the research literature over a ten-year period (2010–2019) seeking to determine how teaching is described in the literature. Descriptions and prescriptive recommendations lifted directly from nearly 500 articles published in 11 of the most highly rated and widely circulated journals over that period paint a cohesive picture of teaching. The research suggests that "teaching" is comprised of thirteen distinct yet interwoven competencies and practices.

The second phase in the development of this map of teaching was data collected directly from the professionals doing the work: teachers. Through a series of interviews, teachers described teaching as they experience it. Their experience ranged from three months to thirty-one years. They teach elementary, middle, and high school students in both core and elective courses. They work in rural, urban, and suburban schools. They reflect a diverse sample of K–12 teachers.

These teachers first described teaching in their own words and also reviewed the results of the review of the research literature to comment on how well it aligns with their own experiences. They concurred strongly: teaching *is* that complex.

As Angela Cochis (high school teacher) put it

> That list IS teaching. Some of these things I do very well. Some I can always get better at. I don't see anything on this list that is not a very important part of teaching. And if you took any one of these things off the list, there would be a problem.

Dr. Lisa Stewart (veteran Advanced Placement teacher in an urban school) asserted "all of this is a part of teaching. It falls apart if you don't have any one of these components."

These are the thirteen competencies and practices identified by the research literature and affirmed by teachers as essential to teaching as they know it:

- Know students. Knowing individual students deeply in a range of dimensions and using that knowledge to drive professional decisions.
- Know the subject matter. Holding, demonstrating, and expanding strong content knowledge.
- Demonstrate pedagogical expertise. Understanding and enacting effective professional practices related to instruction.
- Plan for practice. Routine, strategic, thoughtful planning for both short- and long-term actions.
- Create a learning environment. Strategic, continuous action to create and maintain an environment optimally conducive to learning.
- Engage students in learning. Implementation of activities designed to actively engage students in learning.
- Implement effective strategies. Knowing which specific instructional strategies work well to support learning and enacting them.
- Provide authentic learning experiences. Designing and implementing learning activities that are meaningful and relevant to students.
- Support learning. Identifying and providing a wide range of supports to advance student learning.
- Monitor learning. Actively and continuously monitoring the degree to which students are learning.
- Provide feedback. Continuously providing specific, descriptive, individual feedback to students about their learning.
- Know and follow laws and policies. An active familiarity and compliance with relevant federal, state, and local laws and policies.
- Reflect on practice. A continuous, deep reflection on professional practice for the purpose of improvement.

A visual representation of these thirteen competencies and practices is presented here. The thirteen areas fall into three broad categories: competencies, daily practice, and practice undertaken as often as possible or needed. Teaching is not a linear process so it would be a mistake to think of these actions happening "before" or "after" each other.

As the arrows are meant to suggest, the different competencies and practices interact with each other, reinforce each other, and often occur simultaneously. Like a map, this image is not meant to *duplicate* teaching in faithful detail: there are details, relationships, and interactivities missing; it *is*, however, grounded in the research and affirmed by teachers themselves.

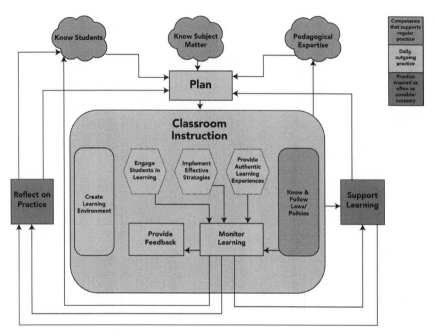

A Map of the Complexity of Teaching. *Source: original digitally created image.*

This book is designed to explore the complexity of teaching. Think of it as a guided tour of teaching for someone considering a career as a teacher or someone outside education but interested to know what teaching is like. Guided tours are not meant to produce expert-level knowledge and they do not try to cover all the details. They provide an *overview* of a place or a topic or a thing; they provide insight. If you are beginning a career in education, if you want to help others understand the profession as you experience it, or if you *are* that other who is seeking to understand, this is your tour. Before we begin, here are some things to remember.

- As we have already said, teaching is not linear. However, to give our tour a structure, the competencies and practices are organized here **very** roughly in this order: pre-instruction, during instruction, after instruction.
- The point of this exploration is not to be exhaustive or authoritative on any part but to sketch the boundaries and provide examples. There's always more and the book will miss things. For example, you will notice that instructional technology does not have its own section. There is no doubt that the skillful use of digital and technological tools is a critical competence expected of teachers but you will find that particular competence embedded in other sections. You might think that issue and others could be framed differently. And you wouldn't be wrong. Exploration, not declaration.
- The content of this book should be used as descriptive, not prescriptive. There is no lack of demand for how teaching should be—and the prescriptive voices are included in the research that undergirds this book. But *please* treat this book as a map—it describes reality. But if your map disagrees with reality, you should accept reality. Description, not prescription.
- Use carefully. This is not a book of formulas, spells, or solutions. No particular results are guaranteed. This book is a map, intended to trace the boundaries of teaching. None of the details here will surprise anyone who is connected to public education; by showing the shape of this vast and complicated thing we call "teaching," perhaps we can be better guided in our thinking and the decisions we make about education.

Are you ready for this tour? Grab your map and let's get started.

Chapter 1

Know Students

Knowing individual students deeply in a range of dimensions and using that knowledge to drive professional decisions

Knowing my students well is probably more important than knowing what in the world I'm talking about, as a teacher. Knowing their names is paramount. I need to know what their families are like, if they have any brothers or sisters. You cannot teach until you have the respect of students and show them that you care enough to know about them and to listen to them. (Rachel Hill, elementary teacher)

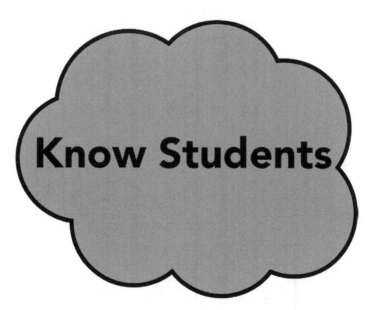

Know Students. *Source: original digitally created image.*

1

Understanding the complexity of teaching requires one to see the entire ecosystem that *is* teaching. There are several components essential to what teaching is that are arguably not the *act* of teaching. These are competencies without which teaching could not happen but which are often excluded from common conceptions of teaching.

These competencies should not be thought of as *prerequisites* to teaching, or something that one must master before teaching is possible. Instead they should be thought of as knowledges that must be continuously refreshed, improved, and expanded in order to support the act of teaching. They are inextricably part of the *process* of teaching.

KNOW STUDENTS

The first of these competencies that teaching includes is knowing individual students deeply in a range of dimensions and using that knowledge to drive professional decisions. For a typical preservice teacher, the bulk of study and preparation probably has in mind classes full of faceless, static students. The human beings so imagined being taught "hold still" in their predictableness, allowing the aspiring teacher to create sample units and lesson plans that were about them and their content knowledge, not about specific learners.

For experienced educators, however, the importance of keeping real, specific students at the center of one's thinking and work is consistently and increasingly obvious. In a real sense, the degree to which a teacher has specific and nuanced knowledge of a student very often has a correlation to the success that student experiences.

WHAT DOES THE RESEARCH SAY?

If the frequency of appearance is an adequate metric, the professional literature between 2010 and 2019 lays a *heavy* emphasis on the importance of teachers knowing students individually and using that knowledge to inform decision-making. The consensus is clear: knowing students is an integral part of teaching.

Research suggests that teachers must reject deficit perspectives of students and avoid making hasty assumptions about them, but instead hold all students to high expectations. Especially important is understanding and valuing students' cultural heritage. This can be done by supporting students in sustaining cultural competence, understanding the relationship between students' culture and worldview and the subject matter, and supporting multilingualism and multiculturalism.

Knowing *about* students is not enough; teachers must build constructive, positive, and caring relationships with students. Recognizing that emotions and learning are inseparable, teachers work to establish trusting relationships with students. At a basic level, this includes behaving unaggressively and avoiding negative interactions with students.

Far from a neutral strategy to enhance learning, "experiencing a positive relationship with a teacher can protect against numerous other negative influences including maladaptive behaviour, negative life events, poor quality child–parent relationships, and referral to special education settings" (McGrath & van Bergen, 2015, p. 13). Teachers must understand the complexity of relationship building and engage students emotionally by addressing their needs, desires, and hopes.

FOR EXAMPLE?

But what does it mean to "know" students? Here is a *partial* list of the ways in which a teacher should know his/her students:

- Know each student's name and how to pronounce it correctly
- Know students' learning status, including progress toward mastery of learning goals, most recent assessment results, and other similar information
- In the same vein, know how much support specific students need in what specific areas of their learning and which strategies for supporting their learning work best
- Know students' learning preferences and tendencies such as which approaches or modalities work best with the *current* group of students
- Know interpersonal dynamics—what groupings of students enhance learning, which students do not work well together, etc.
- Be aware of religious beliefs and observances, particularly those that may interplay with learning and/or school-day routines
- Learn interests and passions *unrelated* to subject matter: athletic and extracurricular involvement, hobbies and passions, and personal interests
- Understand students' biases and conceptualizations of the world, their community, and themselves
- Recognize factors that might place students at elevated risk of discrimination or bullying: physical attributes or limitations, gender orientation, sexual orientation, race and ethnicity, patterns of dress or speaking, dietary habits, religious practices, etc.

There are dozens (if not hundreds) of additional ways in which to know students. The unifying philosophy is simple: teaching is not singular, generic, or passive; it requires a deep and broad understanding of the learner.

IN ACTION

Like teaching itself, "knowing students" is a very nuanced, broad competence. There is not one right or best way to do it. But here is one version of what you might see if you were to watch an educator putting this into practice.

Ms. Spencer stands outside her door during each class change and greets each 9th-grade student by name as they enter the classroom. "Good morning Jamie! What's happening Miguel?" She engages in brief, *personal* exchanges with many of them. "I listened to Beyonce's new song new song last night Dequan; you are right, it *is* crazy awesome! Is your little brother feeling better yet Adonai?"

As the class starts on their bell-ringer activity based on their lab from yesterday, Ms. Spencer circulates among the students, engaging in strategic interactions. She subtly prompts Andrew (who she knows can be absent-minded) to get started on the assignment. She heads off an argument between John and Arturo (neither of whom like to back down if they feel like they are on the losing end of an exchange) by pretending to think the comment John just made to no one in particular was intended for her and not Arturo.

During the discussion about the lab, she does not call on Felicia who is usually an eager participant but has been uncharacteristically silent today—possibly still smarting from last night's soccer loss. A key part of today's lesson is an activity Ms. Spencer added to her plans to address a misconception several students in this class have, based on their answers on yesterday's quiz. Later in the period, Ms. Spencer checks in with Marie and Randy who she is working with on reviewing and mastering several foundational concepts that they should have learned last year.

Knowing that this class can tend to get rowdy if they have an unstructured dismissal, Ms. Spencer is careful to have everyone's attention just before the period is scheduled to end. She fires four or five questions reviewing key concepts from the lesson at what appear to be random students but in fact avoids students who get stressed when they are put on the spot, and—in some cases—recaptures the attention of students who have mastered the content but appear to already be out in the hall in their mind.

Throughout the class *every* action Ms. Spencer takes is informed by her knowledge of *this* group of students and the individual students in the group. Her actions also enhance that knowledge—learning new tidbits about individuals, noticing patterns, and making connections. This knowing of students does not exist in isolation; it provides the framework for her decisions. No two years in her career have been the same because teaching Science is not about vending content knowledge to new customers. It is about brokering and facilitating a connection between the content and the students.

IMPLICATIONS?

It is common for educators to share some version of the claim that relationships with students matter to effective teaching. For example: "Students won't care how much you know until they know how much you care." While there is ample evidence of the relevance to learning of the teacher *creating connections* with students, the competence and practice that subsumes and stretches farther than that is *knowing* students well and using that knowledge to drive professional decisions. The fact of the importance of knowing students has a range of implications.

Preservice teachers: recognize that teaching is fundamentally about *people*. There are many professionals who have deep knowledge in a content area or about pedagogy or some other part of teaching but who are not accomplished teachers themselves because they lack this critical competence: understanding the learner both globally (i.e., what implications does the research on brain development have for how I teach young adolescents?) and personally (i.e., what ought I to do—if anything—with the knowledge that Isabella got in trouble at lunch today?). You cannot prepare for the specific students you will teach before you meet them. You *can* begin to practice applying what you know about people to your decisions.

Teachers: make knowing your students an integral part of your practice. See the pitfalls that come with this. Knowing students is *not* about developing friendships with students. Grave danger that way lies. Conversely, knowing students is not about the collection of data and factoids to insert into a cold mental formula that yields recommendations for optimum decision-making. Knowing a student well allows you to invest more deeply into their learning. Ensuring the greatest possible investment is an act of great care and professionalism.

Administrators: model the process of seeking to know students in your own practice. Your relationship to students is and should be different than that of teachers. But not absolutely so. Knowing students is important to your position as well. Model and nurture practices that seek an ever-expanding knowledge of students—including the multiplicative impact of *teams* of educators collaborating to know and support students and their learning. Explicitly encourage practices that improve educators' knowledge of students.

Consider carefully the feedback you provide about "less rigorous" activities in classrooms, particularly if they are strategically designed. Knowledge gained about individual students in a brief activity can have implications for a teacher's decision-making that significantly improve teaching and learning in the long run.

Faculty members: help preservice teachers view 'knowing students' as an integral part of the process and act of teaching. Provide opportunities to seek knowledge of real students and incorporate that knowledge into practice. The lab setting of teacher preparation programs is well suited both for practice and for meta-cognition about the critical role incredibly variable work plays in accomplished teaching.

WHERE DOES THIS FIT IN TEACHING?

Knowing students is foundational to teaching. A practice that includes the other competencies and practices but lacks a knowledge of students is arguably not really or fully teaching. As this book is focused on K–12 teaching, they may be room for discussion about differences on this point at the post-secondary level. Arguments may perhaps be made regarding whether this applies to online teaching. If these are exceptions, however, they only serve to prove the rule: teaching *depends* on knowing students. Teaching well depends on knowing students (in relevant ways) well.

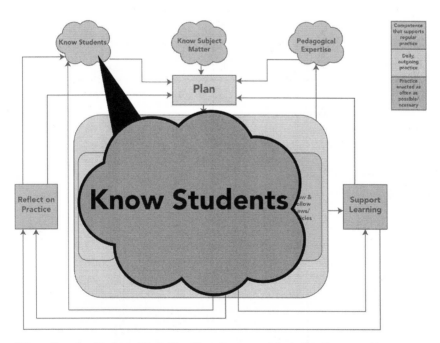

Where Knowing Students Fits In Teaching. *Source: original digitally created image.*

As already argued, teaching is not linear. As such, it is not productive to seek for a "starting place" in the process of teaching. However, the *purpose* of teaching is to affect learning. Knowing the learners should be considered *foundational* to all parts of teaching. The teacher's knowledge of students undergirds and drives decision-making in all parts of the act and the process of teaching. It should be the most significant influence on plans for instruction; it is the basis for the creation of a healthy learning environment; it is what makes efforts toward engagement successful; it drives the selection of the most relevant instructional strategies and learning experiences; and it is the subject of monitoring of learning and the blueprint for providing individualized feedback.

Attempts to support learning that are not based on individual knowledge of that student are sure to be ineffective. Professional reflection that disregards students is likely to lead to decisions that are counter-productive to learning. In order to understand the exceptionally complex whole of teaching, recognize the foundational importance of knowing individual students deeply in a range of dimensions and using that knowledge to drive professional decisions.

Chapter 2

Know Subject Matter

Holding, demonstrating, and expanding strong content knowledge

You can't model something that you don't know yourself. The biggest thing that I have learned about teaching is that you have to be a student as well. I constantly tell my students that I'm still learning things, you know, I make mistakes all the time. I apologize for it. And I move on. You can't think that knowing your subject matter is a matter of getting a degree and moving on. It's an ongoing process. You have *to continue to learn your subject matter.* (Lauren Smith, high school ELA teacher)

Know Subject Matter. *Source: original digitally created image.*

Teachers' level of content knowledge impacts student achievement. In an era where desperation allows schools to assign individuals to teach outside their field of expertise, it is important to remember that content knowledge matters.

Teaching includes holding, actively working to expand, and demonstrating strong content knowledge. Though having deep knowledge of the subject matter one teaches should be an obvious requirement of the job, many employed to teach do *not* have such knowledge. Perhaps that is why the professional literature in the past decade has emphasized an expectation that teachers know the subjects they teach in deep and flexible ways.

KNOW SUBJECT MATTER

It seems obvious. In order to teach something, you have to know it yourself. Less simple is grasping what it means to "know" science. Or math. Or art. Perhaps the answer lies in the training involved in becoming a teacher.

The degree to which teacher preparation programs emphasize content knowledge varies though. Does content mastery mean performing well on examinations? Maintaining a high GPA in courses aligned to a major? In general, certification to teach requires an individual to demonstrate a minimum standard of knowledge in a content area through some combination of successful completion of content courses, subject-area examinations, and teaching practice or internships.

In reality, most teachers develop a deeper expertise in the content they actually teach. Most teaching certificates allow a very wide range of teaching assignments; the more an individual teaches a specific subject, the greater expertise is developed in that narrow area.

WHAT DOES THE RESEARCH SAY?

Beyond mere fact-based knowledge, teachers are expected to know how the discipline they teach aligns with their curriculum in order to more fully know and understand the curriculum itself. As Brent Davis and Moshe Renert put it

> the knowledge needed by teachers is not simply a clear-cut and well-connected set of basics, but a sophisticated and largely enactive mix of familiarity with various realizations of [content area] concepts and awareness of the complex processes through which [learning] is produced.

A key application of this knowledge is in the study and analysis of content standards. For many teachers, effective practice requires the managing of multiple *sets* of standards, skillfully navigating the convergences of them as critical for guiding instructional decision-making. In short, teachers are expected to move well beyond general familiarity to be subject matter experts.

Far from being a universal set of basics, content knowledge is required of all teachers but is itself completely different from one subject to another. Teaching approaches and strategies can be applied across subject areas. But extrapolation and application do not work for content knowledge. Teaching involves a commitment to the ongoing study of the content itself.

FOR EXAMPLE?

Begin by considering the very wide ranges of subject matter that two different teachers can be expected to know based on their teaching certification.

Secondary **science teacher**. Many certification programs certify a secondary science teacher to teach in assignments anywhere from 6th or 7th grade through 12th grade. State grade–level standards vary but here is a partial list of all the *subjects* a secondary science teacher can be expected to know well enough to teach.

- Physical science
- Life science
- Earth and space science
- Biology
- Chemistry
- Physics
- Environmental Science

Each of these subjects includes significant bodies of knowledge—even at the introductory level. Several of them are considered so important that they are often included at both the middle and high school levels (i.e., physical science). A science teacher can be assigned to teach any of these courses (or several at once) whether they have ever taught them before or not. To be a science teacher is to be expected to *know* science.

Elementary **"homeroom" teacher**. Elementary school teachers are generally expected to teach one group of students all the "core" subjects included in the curriculum. Students are expected to develop their understanding of *each* subject area throughout elementary grades. As teachers are typically certified to teach *any* elementary grade level, this means teachers technically must know that entire range of content. This range of content knowledge is likely to include at *least* the following.

- English/Language Arts
  - Mechanics of reading—phonemic awareness, decoding, comprehension, etc.
  - Literacy skills—identifying key ideas and details, craft and structure, etc.
  - Writing—mechanics, craft and structure
- Mathematics
  - Counting and cardinality
  - Operations and algebraic thinking
  - Number and operations in base ten and fractions
  - Measurement and data
  - Ratios and proportional relationships
- Science
  - Motion and stability
  - Earth systems
  - Forces and interactions
  - Earth and human activity
- Social Studies
  - History
  - Geography and environmental literacy
  - Economic and financial literacy
  - Civics and government
  - Culture

These are two examples that are typical of most teaching positions. The same teacher can be assigned to teach college-level calculus to gifted high school students or ratios and proportionality to 6th graders. The same teacher can be assigned to teach six-year-olds (some of whom may never have attended school before) how to hold a paint brush or young adolescents how to create mosaics with broken pottery.

Although this great range of content knowledge *can* be expected of teachers, what is universally required is a strong working knowledge of the content they are, in fact, assigned to teach. For most teachers, this means a commitment to continued development of content-area knowledge throughout their career.

IN ACTION

This book is designed to trace the boundaries of the complexity of teaching. Teaching includes both practices *and* competencies. Knowing one's subject is one of the competencies so it is not an action per se, but here is a quick glimpse of what accomplished teachers do to expand and strengthen their knowledge of the content. How the knowledge is used will be explored in several of the subsequent chapters.

Mr. Lulay found out before the end of the Spring semester that he will be assigned to teach English 10, AP Language, and a writing course for seniors next year. He is already AP trained and has taught that course for several years. It has been a while since he taught 10th grade and he has never taught a stand-alone writing course. This particular course is for students who did not pass the writing assessment the district requires for graduation when they were in 11th grade.

The first thing Mr. Lulay does is study the instructional standards for the English 10 course. In addition to learning goals for students, the document includes a list of recommended literature. Before he leaves for the summer, Mr. Lulay requests copies of the textbooks and teacher materials available for the English 10 course and connects with his department chair to ask about resources and ideas for both classes he has not taught. He joins a group for English 10 teachers on social media, reads (or rereads) each of the pieces he will be teaching from, and begins working to develop a plan for how he will approach each standard.

As part of his planning, he pays particular attention to standard RI10.10, which addresses text complexity. He knows that it is important to provide students with texts on a range of topics, with a diverse array of authors and characters and to support their growth in reading increasingly complex texts. For this reason, he has to spend a great deal of time reading himself. Early in his career he tried teaching a text he had not read carefully and planned for ahead of time. At the end of the unit, he realized how many great opportunities for learning he had missed because he did not know the content well and had to focus on that instead of on strong instructional strategies. This year he invests time in deepening his knowledge of the content.

Mr. Lulay has taught writing as an integrated part of his classes throughout his career and has often worked with students who struggle with writing. He has never taught an entire course on remedial writing, however. How can he assess what his students *have* mastered in the writing process? How do you teach students, who have already been in school twelve years, how to write well? Most of his students are prepared for the writing processes and skills required at the grade levels he has taught. He realizes that he must return to his training on the fundamentals of writing. He contacts a friend who teaches upper elementary and picks her brain about strategies for teaching foundational writing skills.

Throughout the course of the year, Mr. Lulay continues developing his knowledge of the content he is teaching. These new instructional challenges make it necessary to get a firm grasp on concepts he had not had a reason to engage in for many years. By the next year, his confidence level with the content has returned to where it was. His skill set has expanded and his expertise in his subject area is stronger than it ever has been.

IMPLICATIONS?

It is important not to view any of the competencies or practices integral to teaching as more important than the others or to fall into the trap of thinking that it is beneficial to seek to focus on any of them in isolation. They are intertwined and developing competence as a teacher must be seen as a long-range, nuanced process. Content knowledge is perhaps an area that requires balance. Strong competence is critical but not inherently valuable in isolation. There are *many* individuals who are have an unrivaled grasp of their field of expertise but are quite dreadful at teaching the content to anyone else.

Teachers: commit to being a student of your subject. You should be a student of the craft of teaching but continue your search for knowledge in your content area as well. The odds are good that you selected an area because you have an affinity for it. Keep studying. Seek out spaces for ongoing study and discussion. Keep learning. Every bit of expertise you develop expands your ability to serve your students.

Administrators: recognize the importance of teachers expanding their *content area* expertise. When there is so much to attend to in regard to developing and improving instructional practice it can be easy to neglect the development of content knowledge as well. Every content area provides strong organizations designed to support this process. Encourage the teachers you serve to take advantage of such organizations and the resources they provide. Do not take for granted that teachers have learned all they need to know about their content area—or expect them to take care of that learning on their own.

Faculty members: focus on developing the *habit* of continuously developing content-area knowledge. Future teachers are not in your care long enough to learn everything they need to know about their subject areas. Set high expectations for their learning but lay a heavy emphasis on becoming a professional learner. Preservice teachers with long-range commitments to such practice will be well positioned to continue growing throughout their career.

Policy makers: don't focus on content knowledge as preeminent. A strong knowledge of content matter and a willingness to teach do not compensate for inadequate preparation for all the other components of teaching. Instead of focusing only on efforts to recruit professionals already in other fields into education, engage in the work of systematically professionalizing teaching. Students deserve teachers who have very strong content knowledge *and* professional-level expertise in instruction.

WHERE DOES THIS FIT IN TEACHING?

Knowing one's subject matter is foundational to teaching. While there is evidence to suggest that there are other factors that are more closely tied to student success, it is impossible to argue that a person who does not know a thing can teach that thing to another person. Knowledge *matters*. Producing mastery-level learning in students requires deep mastery by the teacher.

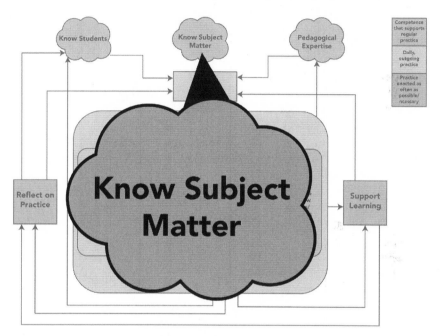

Where Knowing Subject Matter Fits In Teaching. *Source: original digitally created image.*

In this chapter we noticed the very wide range of subject matter that individual teachers can be called on to teach. This does not mean that educators must enter the profession with a deep working knowledge of that entire range of content. It *does* mean that teaching requires a commitment to an ever-expanding expertise in the subjects one teaches. Even areas where one has developed expertise continue to develop over time.

For example, any elementary or middle school teacher who began his/her career recently will have had to adjust their science instruction to account for the downgrade of Pluto from a planet to a dwarf planet. History teachers must continually grapple with how much of modern history to include—by its nature their subject expands every day!

This tour of the complexity of teaching sees it as thirteen competencies and practices that are each distinct but tightly intertwined with the whole. To use the metaphor of a map, knowledge of the content might be viewed as the region that produces the raw material required to teach. The content is the *thing* that is taught. The way in which it is taught, the atmosphere in which it is taught, the manner in which the success of the endeavor is monitored, and other pieces and processes are intricate to "teaching." Without a thing to teach, teaching cannot exist. In order to teach well, the teacher must know the content.

This line of thinking may suggest that the next area to explore should be *knowledge* of effective approaches to instruction. It is reasonable to conclude that knowing how to teach is just as important as knowing what to teach. That conclusion is correct. For the purpose of this exploration, however, multiple pieces of the puzzle are dedicated to the action of teaching. Each includes the embedded assumption of action driven by deep knowledge. Content knowledge requires pedagogical expertise to become teaching. Pedagogical practice requires content to enact. They are intertwined even though they are not synonymous with each other.

Chapter 3

Demonstrate Pedagogical Expertise

Understanding and enacting effective professional practices related to instruction

Accomplished teachers know their students, the subjects they teach, and how to connect those two things in powerful ways. Teachers expertly "diagnose" where their students are academically and "prescribe" the activities and assignments best suited to mastering the content. (Julie Ramsay, middle school teacher)

Demonstrate Pedagogical Expertise. *Source: original digitally created image.*

Teaching includes a grasp of the theory of the work, such as understanding the ways knowledge is produced and knowing the way students think, anticipating common errors and misconceptions, anticipating multiple zones of proximal development, and considering how instruction is likely to impact a variety of students.

As we have already noted, teaching includes both competencies and practices. We explored *knowing students* and *knowing subject matter* and observed that both can be viewed as prerequisites for teaching. While they are not competencies that must or even can be acquired in full before the act of teaching can occur, they are foundational to the process of teaching and equip the individual to act. In this chapter we come to one additional competency that is also foundational to teaching: pedagogical knowledge, skill, or expertise.

Before we go further, let's make sure the terminology does not get in the way of our exploration. In simple terms, "pedagogy" means the art and science of teaching. For the purpose of this exploration of the complexity of teaching when we are trying to understand different pieces that overlap with each other, it may help to think of it as the *theory* of teaching. This part of teaching, then, is understanding how teaching works.

DEMONSTRATE PEDAGOGICAL EXPERTISE

This expertise is complex, requiring that teachers understand a great deal, such as how to make their subjects comprehensible to others, the ways in which knowledge is produced and students learn, and understand student understanding well enough to build models of that thinking. An effective practice relies on student-centered conceptualizations of teaching that view education as transformative.

Effective teaching also requires knowledge of the way students think, including common student errors or misconceptions, an anticipation of multiple zones of proximal development, and a consideration of how instruction is likely to impact a variety of students.

WHAT DOES THE RESEARCH SAY?

The research literature emphasizes that it is essential for teachers to understand the complexity of teaching. As Professor Ann Kipling Brown puts it "skilled teachers know how to relate knowledge of learning theory, subject content and pedagogy into instructional tasks." Although there is no universal methodology for teaching, a wide range of pedagogies or approaches vie for teachers' attention: art-based, practice-lead pedagogy; brain research; passion-led instruction; drama-based pedagogy; and blended learning, just to name a few.

It is important to note that the practices included in this list are *not* equivalent to each other. This is not a list of pedagogies to choose from but a partial list of the many dozens of paradigms for understanding a part, or the majority, of teaching.

In fact, this proliferation of perspective is the reason that a key task for teachers is to sort out how the great mass of research and pedagogical approaches intersect, overlap, and even contradict each other in the development of practice. "Teaching" is not singular nor is there a unified theory or model of what teaching should be. In that context, teachers must make meaning from the existing research, recommendations from peers and researchers, and pedagogical mandates often issued at the school or district level.

The incorporation of digital and technological tools to support learning is strongly emphasized in the literature. Skillful practice in this area requires an understanding of how technology supports content-area learning. Far from simply using mobile devices and social media in the classroom, teachers are expected to consider how to skillfully incorporate various technological applications in support of learning.

Incorporating digital and technological tools into instruction and learning has become such a universal expectation that it is possible to argue that "leverage technology for instructional" should represent a 14th distinct part of the whole of teaching. Indeed, entire fields of research have emerged around promising practices related to the integration of technology. For example, the International Society for Technology in Education, a leading voice in the use of technology to advance teaching and learning, has developed standards for the practice of students, educators, and educational leaders regarding technology integration.

Multiple models for understanding the pedagogy of incorporating technology into teaching and learning exist. Dr. Reuben Puentedura's SAMR model (substitution, augmentation, modification, and redefinition) is wildly popular as an easily understood framework for implementation. Other models, such as Punya Mishra and Matthew Koehler's TPACK (technological, pedagogical, and content knowledge) model are supported by research but less popular with practitioners. While it is clear that teaching now includes a basic expectation for incorporating digital and technological tools, this exploration views that practice as a critical *component* of several of the thirteen competencies and practices.

In regard to pedagogy, it is clear that teachers are very often required to *use* technology and implement digital or technological products in their practice;

such expectations result in far greater benefits to student learning when teachers are able to base their decision-making on a firm understanding of the pedagogy of instructional technology.

A commitment to continuous professional learning is also expected of teachers through such activities as reading professional journals, utilizing a network of professional peers, and giving presentations. For many, schools and districts provide a modest amount of training or professional learning events each year. In some cases, districts support teachers' continued learning in formal contexts such as advanced degrees—through salary raises upon completion and, sometimes, through supporting such professional learning directly. An overarching expectation is for teachers to "ventur[e] into the lost, uncertain and unknown space. Teaching demands a constant negotiation between the lost and found, and dwelling in this space can lead to new exciting curricular and pedagogical possibilities" (Lajevic, 2013, p. 42).

FOR EXAMPLE?

As an exploration of the complexity of teaching, this book is designed to take note of prominent features of the major parts of education without conducting an in-depth study of any. There is certainly no room here even to provide a complete *listing* of the pedagogies of teaching that are supported by research and/or commonly applied to practice. However, the following is a list of some of the pedagogies—or bodies of knowledge about instructional practice.

- Reading instruction—including the whole language versus phonics debate that has raged for decades
- Kinesthetic learning
- Differentiated learning
- Inquiry-based learning
- Game-based learning
- Problem/project-based learning
- Culturally relevant pedagogy
- Reciprocal teaching
- Strategic grouping (whole group, small group, peer group, etc.)
- Grading and assessment
- Collaborative/cooperative learning
- Dialogic, discourse-based learning
- Relationship- and community-building
- Brain development, cognitive load, and brain research
- Experiential learning versus knowledge acquisition

IN ACTION

Like knowing subject matter, pedagogical expertise is a competence rather than a practice. They are also similar in that the purpose of both is to drive decision-making. Pedagogical expertise is enacted through the decisions a teacher makes across the entire span of practice. It is *developed* through ongoing professional learning, application, and reflection.

Teaching is so incredibly complex and there are so many potential paradigms for considering each part of practice that it seems presumptuous to provide an example. Doing so might be akin to deciding which song to sing as an example of *music*. In the spirit of peering in at this part of the complexity though, what follows is a barrage of questions and factors that a teacher might reasonably consider in the course of not more than a day or two. Some integrated into split-second decision-making during instruction and some pondered carefully in the process of planning and reflection.

Mr. Reese has been deeply committed to understanding how teaching and learning work throughout his career. He is particularly interested in how learning occurs, how events and conditions in the classroom interact with the paradigms students carry based on their life experiences, and the very complex issues of race, gender, culture, and other issues that impact students' way of viewing the world and, thus, the way that they learn. As a middle school social studies teacher in an urban school, Mr. Reese teaches a mix of students very diverse in terms of race and ethnicity and socioeconomic status.

Today, Mr. Reese is introducing a unit on the Holocaust. His understanding of how learning works has prompted him to consider a long succession of questions as he plans for this unit and the introductory lesson.

- What is the goal of this unit? Are we aiming for knowledge acquisition, synthesis and analysis, evaluation, or some combination of the above? He settles on this statement as the overarching learning target: *Describe at least three factors that lead to the events now known as the Holocaust.*
- Given this learning goal, what is the best way for thirteen-year-olds to engage with the facts surrounding this historical event? Having seen the efficacy of inquiry-based learning, Mr. Reese designs a series of questions for students to explore using original materials such as newspaper articles, recordings of survivor accounts, letters, memos, and military orders.
- How do I anticipate and plan based on the sensitive nature of this topic? Which of my students may have especially strong reactions to this material? What structures and strategies should I use to ensure that this powerful learning experience does not become counter-productive for any student? Is

the culture of my classroom *really* such that students can engage in difficult conversations and disagree in a way that honors differences?

- How do I structure learning experiences over the course of the unit to ensure that *each* student is learning? What should each student do and what purpose does that action have for their learning, connected to the aims of this unit?
- What evidence of student learning am I looking for? How will I know that a student has mastered the learning target and the standard? What product(s) do I expect from each student and how will I evaluate those products?
- Philippe has just pointed out that there are people who say the Holocaust did not happen at all and asked why we are studying it if it might not have happened. How do I use this question to address the real issue of denying historical events, model how to address difficult questions and objections without relying on my power as a teacher or letting this be about resistance in the classroom?

An accomplished teacher will consider *many* more questions and considerations in the course of a single lesson; these are just a few examples of the reflective process that teachers engage in to apply their pedagogical expertise to decision-making during instruction. The questions asked and answered are influenced by the subject matter at hand, the environmental factors in the particular classroom and community, and the teacher's own paradigms and priorities.

It seems important to acknowledge that there *are* often factors that explicitly block teachers from engaging in decision-making deeply rooted in sound pedagogical expertise. The notion of "teacher-proof" programs or curricula is alive and well even in schools and districts where strong claims of teacher autonomy are belied by the ways in which the teacher actions and expected activities are vigorously inspected for compliance.

The preponderance of research evidence, however, clearly indicates that student learning is best supported by teachers accomplished in their ability to evaluate a range of factors relevant to the learning of the group of students in front of them right now, to consider their rich store of pedagogical expertise, and to make decisions about how best to advance these students' mastery of the learning goals.

IMPLICATIONS?

Developing and demonstrating pedagogical expertise is essential to effective practice. As discussed briefly above, the fact that some individuals working as teachers do not (or cannot) engage in developing and applying pedagogical expertise beyond a narrow band of practice they return to faithfully does more to prove the claim than to disprove it. Recognizing that this practice is integral to teaching has a few implications.

Preservice teachers: don't panic. You do not need to learn the entire theory of all parts of teaching today. Your instructors are doubtlessly working to help you build a solid foundation to prepare you to begin your career. Use these opportunities to learn *how* to develop pedagogical expertise. What you are learning now will serve you well as a beginning teacher; your commitment to *continuing* to learn will heavily influence your effectiveness as a teacher.

Teachers: keep learning. Every group of students you teach is different. There is more to know about teaching than one person can ever learn—what do you not know today that would make a significant difference for future students if you learned it? What emerging pedagogies would benefit your teaching and student learning? Also, resist efforts to deprive you of the opportunity to make decisions about your students. To do so is always frightening but you are a professional educator and should be treated as such. Build such expertise that the box does not fit around you. And help break the box.

Administrators: remember that "why" matters. You have to know the research. Not the vendors' statistics that they call research. Peer-reviewed research by folks only interested in what works and who does the work. "To fidelity" is not a thing. Invest in building the capacity of the teachers on your team. Provide opportunities for them to deepen their pedagogical understanding and build structures that allow (and *expect*) them to apply that understanding.

Avoid shiny objects; you know they *never* have a lasting impact on student learning. At best, they provide a honeymoon spike on a test, gain you credit as a good leader and then ebb when you ride off to your next adventure. Question things. Invest in the long game, in making DNA-level change. A huge piece of that puzzle is in valuing the ability of all teachers to apply deep pedagogical expertise to decision-making then providing the autonomy to make those decisions.

Faculty members: emphasize the ability of preservice teachers to *think*. Students do not need more program implementers; they need professional educators who understand them personally, understand the content deeply, and understand how learning works. Expect your future educators to know the basics but demonstrate their ability to synthesize and apply theories of teaching and learning.

Decision-makers: teaching is incredibly complex and difficult. Don't make laws that rely on narrow mandates. Be part of the work to build educational structures that position teachers as professionals and treat them as such. Professionals are held to very high standards. But they are rarely afforded the dignity of autonomy in decision-making.

WHERE DOES THIS FIT IN TEACHING?

Developing and demonstrating pedagogical expertise is foundational to effective teaching, along with knowing the subject matter. This is the understanding of what works and why. In fairness (as addressed above) there are individuals working as teachers who do not demonstrate deep pedagogical expertise and instead engage in practice that remains that same regardless of the population of students in the room and/or who provide no evidence of engaging in thoughtful decision-making based on an understanding of what works.

Again, the existence of non-examples only serves to underscore the essential nature of developing pedagogical expertise and applying it to teaching and learning. Consider running as an analogy. A great many people run. Significantly fewer understand the existing research on running more efficiently and effectively at the distance they favor and in the terrain available to them. Elite runners dedicate a great deal of time toward understanding the science of running. *Why* a particular stride or posture or diet or shoe has the effect that it does. And they apply that understanding to what they do repeatedly until they have fully parlayed that knowledge into habitual action. Accomplished teaching is similar. It matches theories of teaching with specific circumstances and develops action in response.

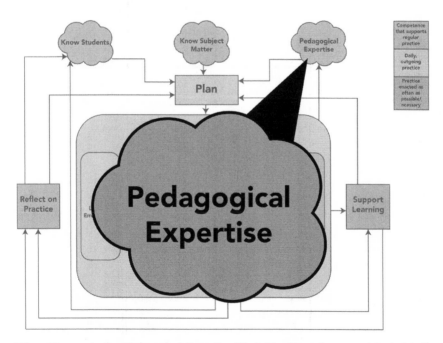

Where Demonstrating Pedagogical Expertise Fits in Teaching. *Source: original digitally created image.*

Knowing students, knowing the subject matter, and demonstrating pedagogical expertise are the three competencies that can be viewed as foundational or antecedent to the act of teaching. They are likely not what most think of as "teaching" but without them, teaching is fundamentally different. They are the "what"; next we begin to explore the "how" of teaching, the actions that form the complex and dense core of teaching itself.

Chapter 4

Plan For Practice

Routine, strategic, thoughtful planning for both short- and long-term actions

You have to plan; if you don't have a plan, lessons will be a disaster. It is important to plan for both the short and long term. I have a daily plan but it's all part of a bigger unit plan. We introduce the unit at the very beginning, so that students know what they're working towards and what the end result is. Then the plan for each day is built on progressing towards those goals. (Brandi Morris, elementary teacher)

Plan for Practice. *Source: original digitally created image.*

This includes lesson, unit, and course planning. Plans should include (but are not limited to) questions to ask, assessments to administer, activities to enact, and contingency plans for when the primary plan does not work the way it was designed.

Although some of the practices and competencies of teaching that we are exploring are generally a mystery to anyone not personally involved in education, the need to plan is one part of teaching that is easier for non-educators to imagine.

Like many other professions, teaching requires skillful review of the current situation (knowing students) and the aims of the process (content knowledge and learning goals) combined with a consideration of how to apply knowledge of the way the process works (pedagogical expertise). By activating these skills in combination, the skillful teacher is equipped to craft plans for what both they (the teacher) and students will *do*.

PLAN FOR PRACTICE

Teaching includes routine, strategic, thoughtful planning for both short- and long-term actions. This process of planning is integral to the work of teaching. It ranges in scope from long-range planning—such as designing a course of study—to intermediate planning—such as units of study within a course—and the standard expectation that teachers create plans for meaningful lessons every day.

Each type of planning requires the application of somewhat different skills. For example, the design of a course may not consider a specific group of students but may imagine a *category* of students—such as a specific age or grade level. Lesson planning *should* always consider the group of students being taught in order to make specific plans that are responsive to students' current learning.

One of the most basic practices required of teachers is the development of detailed, written plans for daily instruction, or "lesson plans." While there are many widely known, evidence-based approaches to planning—such as Universal Design for Learning, the Danielson Framework, and backward planning—there is no *universal* template for approaching the work of developing daily lessons. Generally speaking, however, there are a few elements understood to be part of a lesson plan:

• an explicit statement of the goal of the learning (sometimes called a learning target), linked to a learning *standard*
• one or more activities the teacher and students will engage in to advance learning
• the strategy, approach(es) or instrument(s) the teacher will implement to gauge the degree to which students are progressing toward the learning goal

There are several other elements that often are included in the design of a lesson: the resources required, connections to prior learning, the way(s) in which learning will be approached such as learning and instructional strategies, and several other ways of framing or approaching a part or a combination of the parts listed here.

WHAT DOES THE RESEARCH SAY?

Far from being a simple expectation of the job, the recommendations and expectations surrounding planning are a complex, and sometimes self-contradictory, tangle of minutia. Teachers are expected to identify content to be learned deeply and organize it using a research-based approach, such as the backward-design model. Teachers are expected to ensure that the resulting curriculum follows a logical sequence.

Teachers are not only required to comply with existing, district-level curriculum and plan lessons based on that curriculum, but also to design the lessons they plan based on students' actual misconceptions, while considering those students' cognitive capacity and the cognitive load the planned tasks will impose.

At the lesson level, it is essential for teachers to plan rich and engaging learning tasks that vary in complexity and that prioritize active learning. Also integral to successful planning is the selection of appropriate materials, considering the resources available. Planning must also anticipate addressing multiple student learning outcomes, and supporting a wide range of student responses to learning activities. Teachers must grapple with logistical implementation issues and be prepared but also willing to take risks, thereby demonstrating flexibility and a tolerance for ambiguity in service of deep student learning.

FOR EXAMPLE?

In many schools and districts, the reality is that very few teachers have the opportunity to design an entire course or even units of study. While a deep discussion of the nuance of the concept of a "curriculum" is not within the scope of our exploration, it is relevant to recognize that many districts use state-level learning standards to create more specific guidelines for what students should know and be able to do in each subject at each grade level. It is not uncommon for these documents—called a number of things including "curriculum guides," "pacing guides," and "scope and sequences"—to stipulate which *content* (not only which learning targets) should be taught by teachers and when.

As discussed in chapter 1, teachers are expected to know the students they are teaching well, including the state of their current learning, and to use that knowledge to develop plans for the instruction of those students. It is a fact widely known and acknowledged that students do not learn at the same pace; in spite of that fact however, students are grouped by *age* in school rather than by actual learning progress—with the exception of extreme cases such as when students are made to repeat a grade in elementary school or a class at the secondary level.

In spite of the fact of the great diversity of preparedness and learning progress that is simply part of the construct of schooling, teachers are expected to adhere to the curriculum documents created on the tacit assumption of steady progress throughout the course of a year toward mastery of the course/grade-level learning goals. The overlapping expectation to simultaneously plan and deliver supplemental instruction to support the learning of students who begin or fall behind the proscribed pace will be discussed in more detail in chapter 9.

Teachers are often expected to follow a specific *template* for creating lesson plans. It is not uncommon for the pace of learning to be predetermined and for the format of lesson plans to be predetermined but the responsibility for *creating* the actual plan for learning to rest on the teacher. Perhaps unsurprisingly, it is very common for vendors of instructional resource materials to include sample lesson plans to accompany their products, a feature explicitly marketed as helpful to teachers' planning.

David Holladay, middle school social studies teacher, describes this phenomenon and the position many teachers find themselves in with an extended metaphor.

Miss Smith, you have 30 people coming over for dinner next Friday. Imagine all the things you have do for those 30 people. By the way, once they leave you have 30 more coming into your dining room for you to serve, then 30 more after that. Obviously you have to prepare. Obviously get everything clean. Obviously come up with your plan, create the menu, get groceries, you know, the whole lot of things.

But Miss Smith for the four days preceding this (even though, Miss Smith, you have a master's degree in cooking and been cooking for 20 years, and even though we realize you've have all these people coming over) what we're going to do for the four days preceding is take you somewhere and teach you how to cook. You will get professional development in cooking. Because it looks good. Teaching the cooks how to cook sounds good, plays well.

Does that sound right? Of course not. Turn her lose, let her work and
ize she has got a list of 50 things she has to get accomplished before th,
waves of 30 people come in for dinner. The best thing we can do to hei,
her? Leave her alone and ask her what we can do to help. That imaginary
scenario is what it is really like to be a teacher. It sounds crazy but that's
what it's like.

In spite of this conflict between the expectation to plan and expectation to implement a curriculum—or even a specific commercially produced instructional product—"to fidelity," as David is describing and the deep frustration this conflict can cause, there *are* strong examples of balancing expectations and autonomy. Among the most powerful of these is the collaboration of teams of teachers to examine the evidence of student learning "live" or immediately after it is available and make decisions about how best to drive learning forward in response.

Researchers, such as Jenni Donohoo, advocate for the power of "collective efficacy"—strategic, routine collaborative work by professional educators to make and enact decisions. Many schools and districts prioritize the implementation of "professional learning communities"—formal structures for collaborative work by teachers. In those contexts, planning is delegated to the teacher even when school- or district-level curriculum documents provide the framework for practice.

IN ACTION

Accomplished teachers engage in multifaceted planning, from mapping out the progression of a semester or a year of learning to tweaking plans for the same day in response to new evidence of students' needs or to unexpected events or factors that directly impact learning—like an unannounced change to the schedule, a weather event, or any number of nonacademic preemptings of the usual schedule.

While schools and districts engaged in highly effective practice tap into teacher expertise for curriculum design and course planning, the majority of teachers have limited opportunities to plan at the macro level. Planning is focused heavily at the lesson level. Disclaimer: it is important *not* to conclude that lesson planning is the only or even the bulk of the planning that teachers do. A great deal of noninstructional planning is also required: field trips, activities, special events such as spirit week, schedules, and paperwork. This book is exploring the complexity of teaching, which should not be taken to be the totality of the work that teachers do.

rd's classroom is likely to conclude that she has a
gift for connecting with her kindergarten students.
oom of seventeen five- and six-year-olds is both full of
typical of a kindergarten classroom *and* highly focused
propriate learning—which is difficult to accomplish with
to the customs and practices of formal schooling. Ms. Ford is
a gifted teacher but her ability to impact the learning of her students
so deeply is due to her *planning*.

She begins with a deep knowledge of her subject matter. Through the course of her teaching career, Ms. Ford has worked to deeply understand the way in which the foundational learning intended in kindergarten works. She understands how to make that learning happen as well. She knows how to develop number sense, phonological awareness, and each learning goal she has for her students.

But key to her work is understanding her students. She knows that Drew will want to hop up and come tell her about how Jasmine and Arturo are talking when they should be working and what she needs to say to get him back to his own learning quickly. She knows that Matthew's dad will drop him off late more than once each week and how to get him settled and focused on his learning quickly. She is aware that Raquel grasps new concepts better when Ms. Ford talks her through it personally.

Here is a peek into Ms. Ford's planning cycle. For skillful teachers like her, planning is a complex dance that draws on existing knowledge sets to create a plan for action that is anchored in the big ideas articulated in the state standards, tailored to the specific group of students in her class this year, and flexible enough to adjust mid-week or even mid-lesson.

At the end of each instructional unit, Ms. Ford meets with her grade-level team. They discuss the evidence of student learning that they have, implications for practice based on that evidence and next steps. As a result of those conversations, Ms. Ford blocks out the plan for the next unit by week. Each week, she must submit her plans for the following week to her principal by midday on Friday. She consistently submits her plans but also reviews them over the weekend, adding or adjusting details based on the actual progress students have made.

During her planning period and at the end of each school day, she reviews how the lessons went (as a kindergarten teacher, she teaches math, reading, science and social studies to her students) and adjusts the plans for the following day. This phase of planning is the point at which she gathers and prepares the materials for the following day—tracing pages for the letter "g," safety scissors for the "long e sound" matching activity, counting blocks, glue, crayons, wipes, etc.

She also makes specific plans for how to modify some of the activities for specific students. Dorothy has not mastered scissors yet—how can she participate in the "long e sound" activity without getting bogged down for too long? Frankie makes a huge mess with bottle glue; where is the big glue stick that works for him? But the real magic of her planning is in strategically grouping students for "small group" instruction.

As is common with kindergarten teachers, she works with groups of between three and five students at the point of their greatest learning need throughout the day. Because *everyone* participates in small group instruction, there is no stigma attached to it. Because Ms. Ford is skillful at identifying exactly what each student needs next and who is at a similar place to a few peers, each group's work is different. All that "differentiation" is possible because Ms. Ford *plans* well.

IMPLICATIONS?

At the risk of making the claim cliché, planning is critical to teaching. Planning is the process of synthesizing the teacher's knowledge of students, subject matter, and pedagogy to produce the action steps to be taken by the teacher and the students. It is the bridge between knowing and doing.

The next several chapters will examine the nature of the actions that result from such plans but it is important to note the essential nature of planning. It may be tempting to assume that highly skilled professionals can rely on their experience and knowledge to make decisions at the point of action. Teaching and learning are far too complex for such practices to be effective. While learning is so messy that plans must remain open to adjustment, attempting to teach without a plan is equally likely to produce chaos and a well-ordered but impotent performance.

Preservice teachers: recognize the essential nature of planning. Your preparation program has likely emphasized this part of being a teacher. You may find the activities you have completed to this end contrived. Trust your professors: planning is a skill that will serve you well as a teacher. You cannot know your students before you meet them. You *can* know your subject area and what works pedagogically. If you are prepared to synthesize these knowledge bases with what you learn about your students, your journey to developing accomplished practice is well begun.

Teachers: you do not need instruction on the nature or the importance of planning. But remember that it really is the key to successful practice. Advocate with your administrators and local decision-makers for institutional structures that treat both collaborative and individual planning as the lynchpin to effective teaching and learning. Make the intricacy of that process visible to others and speak for protecting the time and autonomy necessary for planning well.

Administrators: examine the alignment of your knowledge and belief about planning and the structures that you institute. Note, for example, that in high-performing countries around the world, teachers spend a significant part of their contract time each week in planning—for example, teachers in Shanghai spend only twelve hours per week teaching; the rest of their time is spent on collaborative planning. Yes, you face mandates to do more things than can get done and it is very difficult to treat planning for instruction as so important that it must not be interrupted.

Consider what would happen if your school or district placed protections on planning similar to those that already exist. We have "uninterrupted reading instruction blocks" in elementary; what if we *also* had "uninterrupted planning blocks" as well? Who would the primary beneficiaries of such structures be? Students.

Faculty: keep your focus on the importance of planning. Insert activities into your teaching that build this competence in preservice teachers. Even when they are in their early stages and observing, merge those experiences with the (hypothetical) planning activities preservice teachers undertake. Model how to synthesize content knowledge, pedagogical knowledge, and knowledge of students in developing plans. Instead of calling them "sample" lesson plans, perhaps it would assist the process of internalizing this expertise to call them "practice" lesson plans.

Policy-makers: remember that time is the enemy of success in most schools. Take stock of all the requirements that are placed on schools by your decisions; your intentions are good but the actual impact on individual teachers (who ultimately do the bulk of the work required to comply with most such requirements) is to rob them of time essential to planning.

Consider how to design structures that keep the bulk of the extra-instructional tasks away from teachers *and* support school-level structures that prioritize planning. "Giving" teachers a planning period of a minimum number of minutes should not be about the rights of individual teachers. Designing a structure that recognizes that effective practice is not possible without strong planning is about collectively pursuing successful outcomes—in student learning.

WHERE DOES THIS FIT IN TEACHING?

As we have discussed in this chapter, planning is the bridge between thinking and doing, between knowledge and action. Effective teaching relies on strategic action driven by expert decision-making. The process of turning expertise into action is organized by planning. As such, planning is an essential component of teaching. And probably, the practice most likely to be explicitly required of any individual employed as a teacher.

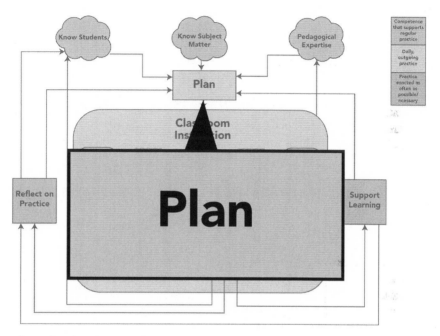

Where Planning Fits In Teaching. *Source: original digitally created image.*

"Those who are victorious plan effectively and change decisively. They are like a great river that maintains its course but adjusts its flow. They are skilled at both planning and adapting"—Sun Tzu.

Chapter 5

Create a Learning Environment

Strategic, continuous action to create and maintain an environment optimally conducive to learning

Teaching is ongoing. I am teaching even when I'm saying nothing. The way that I resolve conflicts or the ways that I handle things in my class that I may not have expected, is an important part of learning—maybe as important as the instruction itself. (Dr. Phil Wilson, music teacher)

Create A Learning Environment. *Source: original digitally created image.*

Teachers nurture a classroom culture that values the individual for his/her uniqueness and prioritizes healthy interactions over social (and antisocial) behavior that would impede learning.

As we continue our tour of the landscape of the competencies and practices that constitute teaching, we come now to the first of the domains that might be conceived as part of the action of teaching. Part of the *act* of teaching or something you could see happening in a classroom if you were to watch teaching happen. Before we dive into this practice, it may be helpful to study the image we have been using to guide our exploration.

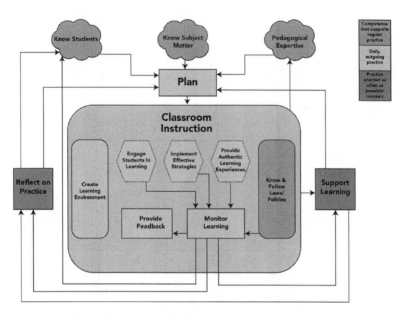

Our Map of Teaching. *Source: original digitally created image.*

At the center of the image is an area labeled "Classroom Instruction." Within it are seven practices that are integral to the *act* of teaching. Four of them are clearly distinct although they are intertwined with the other practices. Three (designated by a dotted outline) are conceived of and will be discussed as different from each other. However, in many ways they are somewhat interchangeable with each other in that it would be easy to use the same example to illustrate more than one of them. More on this later.

Together, the seven practices encapsulate the boundaries of teaching as most think of it—the act of teaching. As discussed in an earlier chapter, it is misleading to think of teaching as linear or sequential. In that spirit, we begin our exploration of the act of teaching with a practice that could be framed as necessary *before* learning can happen but that, in fact, requires continuous action: creating and maintaining an appropriate learning environment.

There is a good chance that someone reading this chapter has scanned the list of competencies and practices and studied the image representing them looking for "classroom management" or "discipline." Those concepts and the practices they describe are indeed an essential practice in teaching but they are just part of a broader set of practices—those designed to arrange the classroom space, set conditions, and create the routines that establish and maintain an environment that encourages and supports learning.

CREATE A LEARNING ENVIRONMENT

Teaching includes strategic and continuous action to create and maintain an environment optimally conducive to learning. Doing so requires attending to a complex range of priorities: creating a space that is emotionally safe; nonthreatening; noncompetitive; actively engaging; flexible, social, and cooperative; motivational; socially and culturally healthy; and inviting to and reflective of the myriad of human relations.

WHAT DOES THE RESEARCH SAY?

A key strategy in nurturing such an environment is striving to meet students' needs for autonomy, competence, and relatedness. Thus, effective teachers support and enhance students' autonomy, teaching them to appreciate and guide their own learning. Equally important, teachers implement strategies that value and promote self-discipline, creating conditions for students to co-create the culture of their learning environment. Student professionalism is fostered as students are assisted in monitoring and regulating themselves.

Effective teachers employ effective management skills by finding a balance between unlimited freedom and excessive structure. That balance is enhanced by providing a clear understanding of behavioral expectations and norms; modeling respectful behavior; and invoking and applying routines in creative, improvisational ways. Teachers avoid coercive practices, acting instead as a warm demander through a relational approach to management of the learning environment. Teachers respond to students who exhibit behaviors disruptive to the learning environment first with small corrections and interventions for improvement instead of attempting control via threats.

The preservation of a healthy learning environment is often the result of a healthy ecosystem of interactions, particularly one that values democratic interactions. Students are allowed voice and choice, having been passed control from the teacher. When certain tasks are mandatory, the teacher provides rationales and the opportunity for co-development of procedures. Learning is positioned as a co-investigation of the world by teachers and students, a process that values risk-taking, encourages individual reasoning, and prioritizes equity and access.

In nurturing a healthy learning environment, teachers eliminate gender stratification and segregation, attend carefully to and avoid racist constructs, strongly root out any form of harassment, and ensure student safety. Individual practices that promote a positive environment, such as playing music, allowing students access to water, incorporating movement and activity breaks, and strategically organizing the room, are blended and incorporated in ways that best serve specific cohorts of students.

FOR EXAMPLE?

It may be helpful to think of *creating a learning environment* as doing the work of setting the *conditions* that make it most likely that students will learn well. The importance of attending to the learning environment is tied to the fact that students are humans—varied, impulsive, curious, well capable of boredom, and not uniformly the same in a thousand other ways. Keep in mind that the entire notion of school is an attempt to tame the wild nature of learning and apply it evenly to learners who themselves are not passive vessels into which knowledge can be poured.

Classroom management, discipline, classroom culture, and a bevy of other ideas related to creating and maintaining a learning environment all exist as entire fields of study. Most teachers have had some (if not a great deal of) required professional learning on this practice. Here are just some of the categories or questions to consider.

- How should the seating in my classroom be arranged? Should I assign seats in my classroom and (if so) how do I decide who should sit where?
- What should I put on the walls of my classroom? Student work? Posters with subject matter or inspirational quotes? How much is enough or too much?
- Assuming I can control the lighting in my room, what should I do? Does the warmth of the light matter? Does natural light matter?
- Assuming I can control the temperature in my room, what should I do? What temperature is the right balance between "cold-natured" and "hot-natured" students? Does room temperature have any effect on learning?
- What routines should I establish in my classroom? What should be as-needed and what should we do every day, no matter what?

- What is my procedure for addressing requests to go to the bathroom, nurse, counselor, office, other-place-not-the-classroom-I'm-supposed-to-be-in?
- Should I allow students to eat and drink in my classroom? If so, how does that work?
- How are students expected to address each other? Me?
- How do I get students to participate actively? How do I deal with teasing?
- What do I do when a student or students are talking when they should be listening?
- What do I do when a student refuses to follow my directions? Leave the classroom without permission? Curse a peer? Curse me?
- What is the difference between banter and bullying? Where is the line between playing and fighting?
- Should I play music in my classroom? Should I allow students to listen to their own music?
- How much freedom do students have to make small decisions without my permission—throw away some trash, get a drink, take something across the room, etc?
- What strategies will I use to make *sure* I am not calling on individual students or groups of students more than others?
- How do I explicitly include students in the development of norms and procedures for our classroom?
- What can I do to create an atmosphere that prioritizes learning over compliance and control?

The fact is that this part of teaching alone is complex. Creating a learning environment is *not* as simple as drafting a list of rules and decorating a bulletin board. The atmosphere of a classroom is a living, active, fragile thing that requires continuous nurturing to stay healthy. Even an environment that is very healthy can be damaged or threatened by events outside the control of the teacher or the students.

Part of the great complexity of teaching is that the majority of its component parts are themselves complex and require both a commitment to deep learning and experience to develop expertise. Successfully blending these distinct competencies and practices with each other is also a skill worth noting that we will not have time to explore. As one's knowledge and understanding in a particular area grows, adjusting practice in that area ripples into other areas of intertwined practice.

IN ACTION

Mr. Bogert's teaching assignment says "5th grade" and the subject he teaches most is math but his focus is almost always on maintaining the learning environment he has worked so hard to create. As an accomplished teacher, Mr. Bogert spends a great deal of time at the beginning of each year getting to know his students: their personalities, preferences, peeves, and the peers they get along with and those they don't. He has learned a lot about young adolescents through his experiences as a teacher and through his study but his general knowledge of "what works" for students of this age is not enough—he has to know how that knowledge applies to the students in his classroom *this* year.

The room students step into each day is designed to be welcoming and focused on mathematical thinking at the same time. There are two couches, a table with wobble stools, a section with four canvas chairs, tables, and a few individual desks. Seating is assigned but rotates frequently with student input. Mr. Bogert has several lamps in his room and often leaves his overhead (florescent) lights off. Two of the walls are covered with student work. One wall has a huge section painted to function as a dry-erase board. Students frequently use that space to work together on problems they are tackling.

At the start of each year, Mr. Bogert invites students to work together to decide how their classroom will work. He often has to nudge students away from the very strict set of rules they think of on the first draft. The classroom is a manifestation of the deep dignity with which Mr. Bogert treats each student— even when they are wrong or have violated the class's compact for behavior. Students are also expected to treat each other with dignity and they do. They understand that Mr. Bogert's class is about learning, not about him. The boundaries they set for themselves are designed to protect each student's learning.

As part of his regular routine Mr. Bogert places a phone call to each student's house at least once a month, making several calls each week. The purpose of the calls is to establish a relationship of trust with the parents. In each call, Mr. Bogert provides a brief, personalized report about the student's progress in his class. He makes a point of noticing something admirable the students have done and including those details in his calls–often choosing whose house to call based on who is setting an example, making great improvement, or otherwise upholding the culture the class works together to maintain.

Being human (and young adolescents at that), Mr. Bogert's students do mess up. Because he understands the impact of brain development and executive function on students at this age, Mr. Bogert is very careful never to correct students out of frustration. More often than not, simply calling a student's attention to their actions and asking them to describe those actions in the context of the class's compact is enough for the student to recognize the problem and correct it themselves. Mr. Bogert is also fond of using proximity as a subtle cue to students to pay attention to what they are doing.

Mr. Bogert does write disciplinary referrals and call parents about inappropriate behavior. But both happen less frequently than they did before he began to view maintaining a healthy learning environment as an act of cooperative creation, not something the teacher does to or even for students.

IMPLICATIONS?

While the value of student input is clear, there is a clear opportunity for **preservice teachers** to begin considering what their position or preference is on a range of the questions raised in this chapter along with others. The point applies to many other parts of teaching but it is important to note that copying another teacher's approach to creating a positive learning environment is unlikely to be effective. It is healthy to emulate parts of the practice of accomplished teachers but keep in mind that your practice has to align with your philosophy, your strengths, and your knowledge. It would be worth your time to imagine and plan out this part of your practice now. Yes, it will evolve as you gain experience as a teacher but there is no reason not to wrestle with these questions before you have your own classroom.

Teachers: keep your eye on the ball. Classroom management and discipline are not about control; they are about keeping space clear for learning. Consider that school and classroom rules have very little value on their own; above all else, work to keep the enforcement of rules from blocking students from learning.

Beware also of teaching unintended lessons. And give yourself some grace: you are attempting to guide and moderate the actions of young humans. They can be *so* frustrating and unpredictable; but they are worth it! Your ability to create and maintain an optimal learning environment is directly tied to your ability to connect with them. Put in work to understand and know your students and invest in building a shared culture; if they have a safe and inviting space to learn, your students will help protect and sustain it.

Administrators: there are whole conversations to be had about issues connected to this. For now, let's focus on the implications as they relate to teachers. Value culture over compliance. You are a highly trained professional educator; you don't need your teachers to all do the same thing—you need them to all pursue a high bar of excellence. Support teachers' work to create strong learning environments. Get them different furniture if they want it. Paint their classroom funky if that helps. Encourage them to invest time in developing relationships, norms, and procedures—every minute spent at the beginning of the year building that environment will save at least 10 minutes of distraction from learning later in the year.

A strong word here for **faculty** of teacher preparation programs. This is one of the areas in which beginning teachers are most often mostly or completely unprepared. Preservice teachers do not need a single class period of instruction on developing strong classroom environments; they probably need an entire course. The research on what works is readily available. Incredible examples of how to put these ideas into practice exist all over the country.

We know that figuring out classroom management, student discipline, creating a learning environment—whatever you want to call it—we know that figuring this out is routinely the difference between surviving the first few years of teaching to remain a teacher and leaving the profession. Very few beginning teachers leave the profession because they do not have enough content knowledge or cannot plan effectively; it is very often a frustration tied to their struggle to get a handle on student management. Make the development of this expertise a priority!

WHERE DOES THIS FIT IN TEACHING?

Creating a learning environment is a key part of teaching. It can and does include actions taken outside the act of teaching—such as arranging the physical space—but the work of establishing and maintaining a positive learning environment is an ongoing process. The learning environment includes the physical, the mental, and the emotional space of learning. These are all impacted by the actions of the teacher and the students.

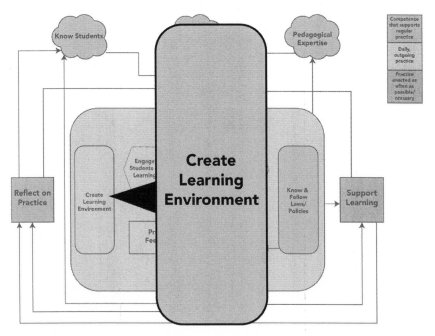

Where Creating A Learning Environment Fits In Teaching. *Source: original digitally created image.*

While the interactivity of the learning environment with other parts of the act of teaching is not noted on our graphic, there is interplay. There is a reason restaurants and hair salons and airports put a lot of thought into their decorations, the patterns of behavior of their employees, the lighting, the music. None of these things are the products or services customers come to those places to get. But they are a factor in the decision clients make to keep coming back to those places and to express satisfaction. In a similar way, managing and maintaining a healthy learning environment is critical to learning and is a key component of teaching.

Chapter 6

Engage Students In Learning

Implementation of activities designed to actively engage students in learning

I'm always looking for more ways to better engage students that are effective and meaningful. It takes planning activities that focus on collaboration, are challenging, and are best for their learning. Learning is not passive receiving of information, learning is active. *And it's my job to have a plan to make that action happen.* (Angela Cochis, world language teacher)

Engage Students in Learning. *Source: original digitally created image.*

Teachers set high expectations for all students through a variety of means including the design and implementation of interesting, cognitively demanding learning activities. Teachers make students active participants in their own learning.

Teaching includes the implementation of activities designed to actively engage students in learning. In some ways, the next three chapters encompass what those lacking a deep familiarity with the complexity of the profession likely think of as "teaching." They could all reasonably be placed under the umbrella heading of "instruction."

However, the range of competencies and practices is so broad that these three categorizations serve to illuminate the overall complexity by providing substructures through which to understand it. Because they are so intertwined, there is no obviously correct place to begin the exploration. With apologies to those who might prefer another area of practice, we begin first with student engagement in learning.

ENGAGE STUDENTS IN LEARNING

It seems so obvious as to be strange to mention—learning requires the learner to participate in the process; a teacher cannot learn for a student. On the other hand, who has not experienced a class or presentation from which it was difficult to derive any new knowledge or understand because it was so dry, so inept at engaging one's attention or imagination? Yes, the learner must muster the will to participate in the process and must choose to engage; however, the responsibility for designing and setting conditions to invite and motivate such participation rests with the teacher.

The antecedent professional practice to engaging students in learning is the development of high expectations for all students, including the belief that all students are able and willing to engage in challenging instruction. Teachers must examine their expectations of students in order to clearly communicate an expectation of growth from every student.

In setting challenging learning goals, teachers explicitly communicate high expectations for all students—particularly those historically marginalized in the context of school. But demanding much of students is merely the beginning, not the essence of learning. Learning is a demanding, complex, wonderful process. Framing it as such and offering students opportunities to participate actively in that process—instead of passively receiving knowledge infusions from the gurus who deign to bless them with it—is an important part of effective teaching.

WHAT DOES THE RESEARCH SAY?

High expectations for learning are manifested in the engagement of students in interesting, challenging intellectual work. Far from simple, such practice requires teachers to "work against the grain" (Neumann, 2013, p. 310) of existing student assumptions and learning habits, keeping them engaged in the learning process and striving to transform knowledge sources into meaningful learning.

Meaningful engagement in learning is itself motivating to students. Examples include deconstructing complex ideas, problem solving, exploration of students' interests, and relevant, real-world learning.

To make engagement possible, teachers must develop a number of skills in students including careful and logical thinking; creative thinking; metacognition; and the ability to plan, monitor, and evaluate their own learning. Students also must be taught to develop a synthesis of findings, engage in active participation in structuring and displaying data, and publicly defending and debating ideas.

The importance of student engagement is simultaneously so obvious as to be unremarkable and so complex as to be difficult to adequately explain. It requires physical activity but is not satisfied by it. It insists on deep and careful thinking but expects more than thinking alone. The deep and active engagement of students in their own learning is one of the pillars of teaching.

FOR EXAMPLE?

It might be tempting to oversimplify this practice to "make kids do work." There is a difference, though, between a room full of students dutifully completing tasks assigned to them and students deeply and actively engaged in learning. This engagement we speak of is both the application of one's *mind* to the subject at hand and the employment of one's body to participate in the activities designed to produce learning—in other words, the involvement of one's whole self in the process of learning.

This is no simple matter. In fact, it is exceptionally tempting to create "assignments" for students that focus on compliance and completion. Deep learning is messy and much more difficult to shepherd than the disconnected completion of "work." Engaging students deeply in the process of learning requires a synthesis of the concept and/or content, how that concept/content is best learned, and an understanding of the students themselves.

Note that student engagement does not mean that the teacher is not involved, or indeed directing the learning. The idea is that the presence of the body of a completely or mostly passive student does not do much for that student's learning. Learning must be active and students must be directly involved in the process for it to provide value to them.

As we have pointed out, this is not an exhaustive study of teaching nor a manual for doing the work but an exploration of the reality of teaching. What follows, then, are a number of examples designed to illuminate what student engagement can look like. Some are accompanied by examples of practice that reflect low student engagement, for the purpose of illustrative contrast. Let's look into a classroom where students are engaged in their learning now.

- Students are alert and track the person speaking with their eyes. Their attention is on the speaker, instead of being distracted by anything else.
- The teacher pauses regularly to ask questions designed to determine how well students are following the line of thinking. The teacher may have a strategy for ensuring that she does not call on the same few students every time.
- Students take notes or complete quick writes—short journal-type responses to prompts specific to the topic/idea. For example, "Why did some of the frogs muscles respond to stimuli? What does that suggest about how muscles work?"
- Students ask and answer questions related to the content in a variety of contexts. Socratic seminar, whole- or small-group work, etc.
- Students engage in the learning together. Think-pair-share, cooperative learning, reciprocal teaching, and similar strategies are designed to encourage collaborative learning. Classroom norms ensure that students remain engaged in the work even when the teacher is not directly supervising their group.
- Learning may be structured around one or more larger paradigms, each of which has high student engagement as a major aim.
  ◦ Service-based learning. Content-area learning enacted through the identifying and addressing a real need or issue in the community.
  ◦ Inquiry learning. Students tackle an open question or problem, collecting evidence to support a proposed solution.
  ◦ Project-based learning. Students engage in an open-ended question related to the learning goals. The ways in which they pursue deeper learning are flexible.
  ◦ Gamification. A lesson, unit, or entire course is designed to motivate student participation and engagement by adopting the principles of game-play such as badging and leveling up. Perseverance toward the

goal (learning) is valued rather than the simple completion of uniform tasks.

While teaching and learning do not exist in binary, black and white practice, it is also not difficult to provide contrasting examples between engagement and non-engagement.

- Students who are actively engaged can explain what they are doing and why. Students who are not engaged generally cannot explain why the activity is taking place.
- Students who are engaged are alert. Disengaged students have side conversations, do any number of things *not* related to the learning, are unfocused, or even asleep.
- Engaged students can and do talk about their learning. Disengaged students may complete their assignments but do not have a reason to talk or think about them.
- It is much more common for students actively engaged in their own learning to produce original, meaningful work. When the focus is on learning instead of doing, the doing yields more substantial evidence of learning.
- It is often possible to *feel* the energy in a classroom full of engaged students. The body language of the individuals, the tone of voices, the observable actions all signal keen attention to the learning. The energy of a disengaged classroom is also palpable: flat, silent, or chaotic.

FOR EXAMPLE?

Beware of formulaic approaches to engagement. It can be tempting to reduce this practice to a mathematical construct—how many different students answered a question today; did the students at the front of the room pay attention better than the student at the back of the room; how many students engaged in off-task behavior, etc. Any one of these questions and others like them could be a valuable *part* of reflecting on engagement. But engagement is not as simple as improving the statistics. Engagement is nuanced and variable. As with the other parts of teaching, it requires specific attention and the development of expertise over time.

Mr. Roncoroni places a very high premium on engagement in his world language classes. He stresses to his students that learning is about mastering and *using* new knowledge and skills. Sometimes it can be easy to forget that he teaches world languages because most of the activities that happen in his classes are designed to get his students to learn, read, and speak Spanish— instead of completing activities *about* Spanish.

While Mr. Ronocoroni uses a range of strategies to keep students actively engaged, there are five rules he has made for himself to stay on target.

1. Make it real. Early in his career Mr. Roncoroni found a connection between the way children learn words in their native language and the way language learners learn words in a new language: labeling. Very young children can learn words and learn to *read* if they see the word associated with an object they know. This is why almost everything in a kindergarten classroom is labeled. Using that same approach, one of the first activities each class of students does is to label everything in the classroom. Then as they discover topics or objects they need to reference—even things outside the classroom—they add those labels. Eventually, there are words everywhere for students to reference. As students begin to *use* those words on a consistent basis—saying "¿Puedo ir con la enfermera?" instead of "May I go to the nurse?"—the labeling becomes less important, exactly as it does for a child learning new words.

2. Make it relevant. Although Spanish language acquisition is the goal of his classes, students study topics that are highly interesting to them and that they already know something about. For example, students frequently conduct mini-research sessions or scavenger hunts *in Spanish* about music, movies, or popular culture personalities. Assignments are also frequently tied to issues that are personally important to students such as the curfew for teenage drivers the city recently passed and the state's decision to make girls flag football a sanctioned high school sport.

3. Give students voice. Students have the opportunity to select the details and sometimes the entire assignment or project they complete. This sense of agency in their work is usually motivating to persevere when the tasks get difficult or frustrating.

4. Read, write, and speak in Spanish. These are pillars of language instruction anyway but Mr. Roncoroni works hard to make these standards come alive. His students have access to several magazines and newspapers and a huge digital collection of music, all in Spanish. The student computers in the classroom have Spanish as the default language to encourage students to conduct searches of sites in Spanish, instead of English. Students present their findings, solutions, and proposals in Spanish. Every student is expected to tell Mr. Roncoroni *in Spanish* one thing he/she learned or discovered every day.

5. Model. Mr. Roncoroni speaks Spanish to his students most of the time. They are allowed to ask him questions in English when they do not have the vocabulary they need but he responds in the target language. He does provide a word or two in English as a clue when students get stuck and

he is very animated, using nonverbal communication to support their comprehension. By raising the cognitive demand for students, he keeps them mentally engaged while they are in his class.

IMPLICATIONS?

Even a cursory study of the history of education in the United States reveals that public schooling borrowed heavily from the paradigms and approaches that worked for industry. In particular, a great many structures within schools have long been modeled on what factories are designed for: a place where additive, incremental processes accumulate to the desired product. In this way of thinking, compliance was the key. Students were expected and required to do what they were told to do; with an emphasis on doing.

But as public education begins to understand the ways in which this model does not work for children and to move away from them, our very understanding of learning is changing as well. Learning requires the participation of the learner; yes, the teacher must teach, but *I* must learn. I must *engage* in the process. When my engagement increases, the likelihood that I obtain a deep level of mastery also increases.

Administrators: be careful what you ask for. It is easy to send the message that the show is the thing. This chapter is not titled "Create fun-filled photo ops." The goal is always student learning; activities that make a splash but are light on substance are not valuable to student learning. Also be very careful not to send the message that all disengagement is due to poor practice by the teacher. Sometimes students fall asleep in class because they are not getting enough sleep at night, not because the lesson is unengaging. Sometimes Jason cannot tell you about the learning target for the day because he is upset about what happened at lunch. Value engagement designed to draw students into meaningful participation in their own learning.

Faculty: continue your focus on engagement as key to learning. Provide preservice teachers the opportunities to practice a wide range of strategies and approaches to nurturing active engagement.

Preservice teachers: dig into the question "how will I get students to move beyond participation to *engagement*?" Look for examples in your observations. What do your mentor teachers do to spark that engagement—beyond literally telling the students to do something? Learning happens in the mind and is not passive. Begin building your expertise in drawing students into the process.

Teachers: don't lose sight of the importance of student engagement. Forgive this admonition; yes, it seems silly to even say. But teaching is exhausting and compliance is *much* easier to achieve than rich engagement. Persevere in this area though. Avoid the trap of thinking that "doing" equals learning; specifically that the production of "work" that requires little cognitive engagement has value to students at all. Besides, students are humans and genuinely really do prefer meaningful, engaging learning activities—even if their humanness also makes them seek the path of least resistance.

WHERE DOES THIS FIT IN TEACHING?

Engaging students in learning is one of the most obvious parts of teaching. To the untrained observer, engagement is still visible. Students must *do* things in order to learn. But engagement is far more complex than causing students to complete tasks. It involves enacting skillful, careful plans to draw students into mental contact with the ideas and content and into the enactment of activities designed to nurture, build, and sustain that thinking.

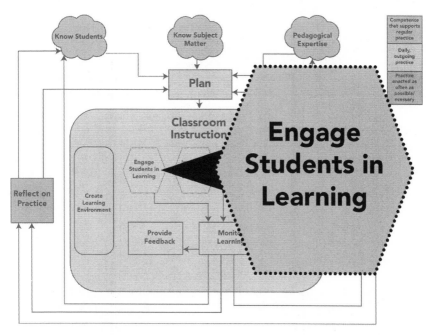

Where Engagement Fits in Teaching. *Source: original digitally created image.*

Most humans display great interest in at least one topic. When presented with the chance to dig deeper into that topic and learn more about it, we enthusiastically do so. But there are many hundreds of topics that an individual is not passionate about. This part of teaching is mastering the practice of tapping students' learning mechanisms and practices no matter what the topic may be. Animating the process of learning in order to advance each student toward mastery of the content.

Chapter 7

Implement Effective Strategies

Knowing which specific instructional strategies work well to support learning and enacting them

It's a simple concept. Instructional strategies are the tools a teacher uses to reach kids. And it is important to have many strategies in your toolkit. You can't screw in a screw with a hammer! (Todd Bloch, middle school teacher)

Implement Effective Strategies. *Source: original digitally created image.*

Teaching is not the implementation of any *particular* strategy, but the expertise to decide *which* strategy to implement under any given set of circumstances.

The second of the three practices that make up the heart of what is most easily understood as teaching is implementing activities designed to produce learning in students. In the United States there is no universally prescribed way to teach anything; in fact there is ongoing and vigorous debate between researchers and practitioners alike about which strategy is better in a number of areas, such as reading instruction. In many cases, it is up to the individual teacher to determine which approaches to teaching or "instructional strategies" work best in their classroom.

There are hundreds, if not thousands, of strategies designed to address a massive variation of situations each of which considers at least one specific factor that impacts student learning: age, content area, student preparedness relative to the learning goal, cultural factors, and many more.

Imagine the concept of "instructional strategies" being a vast warehouse filled with row after endless row of towering shelves, packed full of individual approaches to instruction. There are entire sections that include a multitude of variation on a topic—such as effective questioning. If the last chapter described the answer to the oversimplified question "what should students do?", this chapter explores the answer to the question "what should the teacher do?"

IMPLEMENT EFFECTIVE STRATEGIES

Teaching includes knowing which specific instructional strategies work well to support learning and enacting them. While the active engagement of students is essential to learning, effective teaching also requires that the teacher plan and implement activities in which to engage.

Content-area standards serve as the starting point and driver of instruction aimed at immersing students in that content. To that end, teachers must use a variety of instructional strategies, particularly those which focus or probe student thinking. These student-centered tasks should span multiple levels of cognitive proficiency while providing both enjoyable and effective learning experiences.

WHAT DOES THE RESEARCH SAY?

The effectiveness (and therefore advisability) of a wide range of strategies is supported by research. Among these are those best used at the beginning of class such as bell ringers and posting and discussing standards. Others center on strategies for instruction: explicit instruction, lecture, project-based learning, guided instruction, and teaching with literature. Other strategies revolve around engaging students: concept mapping, reciprocal teaching, inquiry-based learning, games, memorization, writing activities, and many more.

It is well beyond the scope of this exploration to examine the relative impact of these strategies on learning as others have done. However, the short list of instructional strategies above serves to illustrate that teaching is not singular but immensely complex even within specific subdivisions of the complex whole. The understanding and skillful implementation of this wide range of strategies requires a high degree of professional competence as teachers "operate within a high-pressured context, in which the superior memory, complex yet accurate manoeuvers and fast decision-making that characterize expert performance are a real advantage" (McIntyre, Mainhard & Klassen, 2017, p. 42).

The research literature places a special emphasis on collaborative, small-group learning. Teachers are expected to strategically assign students to cooperative groups and prepare them for group work by clarifying the relationship between individual student reasoning and collective practice.

In order to maintain high-functioning student groups, teachers must notice groups' individual characteristics, privately elicit feedback about collaborative work, and strategically change group composition on a regular basis. Making collaborative groups work requires the investment of time and energy by actively developing the necessary skills and practices in students and by setting learning tasks and challenges that are virtually impossible for a student to solve alone.

FOR EXAMPLE?

Let's circle back to the metaphor used above. The fact of a huge warehouse of resources available for a job can be equally reassuring and intimidating. The great news is there is so much to choose from; but it can also be nerve-wracking to have so many choices. For the purpose of getting a better picture of this part of teaching, let's take a look at a list of just *some* of the strategies and groups of strategies that can be used as part of the act of teaching. This list is limited to strategies that have been tested by research. It is important to note that not all instructional strategies that are popular or widely used *are* research based.

• Setting and communicating learning goals

- Direct instruction (a lecture is a form of direct instruction)
- Discovery-based teaching (allows student control through inquiry and hands-on exploration)
- Inductive teaching (teacher demonstrates or provides a model; students infer the "rule")
- Cooperative learning—Jigsaw method (makes students depend on each other), Think-Pair-Share, Three Minute Review (groups review what has been said then ask and answer questions)
- Scaffolding (providing significant supports for working through a specific learning process; supports are withdrawn incrementally as students gain competence)
- Reinforcing effort, affirmation
- Non-linguistic representations—graphic/advance organizers, concept maps, mental pictures, realia or concrete representations, kinesthetic activity, etc.
- Summarizing and note-taking
- Guided or directed thinking
- Anticipation guides—used to activate prior knowledge and build curiosity about a topic. That is, KWL charts (know, want to know, learned)
- Individualized instruction—one-on-one and paced to the specific learner
- Close read—careful reading and rereading of a text, making observations in order to draw conclusions and understand the ideas in the text
- QAR (question/answer relationship)—students learn to distinguish between *types* of questions in order to moderate their strategy for seeking answers
- Document-based questioning—an approach to social studies/history that involves examining and responding to open-ended questions about the document(s)
- Number talks—students solve mathematical problems in multiple ways and share their thinking out loud
- SIOP (sheltered instructional observation protocol)—framework for designing and delivering instruction in ways that are comprehensible to language learners
- Discussion—Socratic Seminar, gallery walk, affinity mapping, concentric circles, fishbowl, hot seat, snowball discussion, four corners/sides, etc.
- Structured academic controversy—similar to a debate, students research one of several points of view and communicate findings in a structured format
- Jumble summary—a review activity where students work to put steps, events, or stages in their correct order
- Learning centers—most often used at the elementary level, stations designed for individual or small groups of students to work through independently or semi-independently, often with review/reinforcing learning activities

Again, this represents a very small sampling of the instructional strategies that have been confirmed as effective by research. And teachers frequently use strategies that are *not* research based that but that result in positive outcomes for student learning.

One of the cognitive tasks for a teacher is to manage the selection of strategies effectively. In addition to the match between the learning target and the state of students' learning, teachers also consider the familiarity of the strategy itself to students. Each of these approaches require the teacher to teach the students the protocols for *doing* the strategy before they can use it. When a teacher plans each lesson, he/she must also factor the question of whether or not the students are familiar with the strategy into his/her planning.

INSTRUCTIONAL TECHNOLOGY

Today, the expectation for teachers to implement digital and technological tools for teaching and learning is so ubiquitous that it would be easy to argue for that practice to stand alone as an essential part of teaching. Spending on educational technology continues to rise, with more than one *billion* dollars spent in 2019—before a spike in spending on devices and infrastructure to address the COVID crisis in 2020 and 2021.

Still, this practice should be seen as *part* of the discussion about effective instructional strategies, not its own domain for two reasons. First, access to digital and technological tools for learning still varies wildly across the country. In some cases, funding is so meager that purchasing and maintaining technological devices or programs at any meaningful scale is simply impossible. How can a specific subset of practice be considered endemic to teaching when the very possibility of engaging in that practice is so tenuous in significant parts of the country?

Perhaps more relevant to the nature of this book's discussion is that the use of technology for its own sake is antithetical to the purpose of its presence in schools in the first place. Technology should be an amplifier and facilitator of effective practice. However, it *does* have its own body of research and does require expert thinking and action. So we explore it briefly here as a subset of strategies for effective instruction.

The use of digital and technological (i.e., electronic) tools for teaching and learning is not new. In fact, the evolution of the tools for the work of teaching and learning mirrors progress in other fields. Typewriters and mimeograph machines have given way to desktop computers and copy machines; cloud-based computing is fueling serious efforts by teachers and schools to "go paperless."

With the spread of the use of technology in schools has come accompanying research and the development of frameworks to guide "tech integration" into the routines of teaching and learning. Some frameworks, such as the SAMR (substitution, augmentation, modification, redefinition) model are very popular with teachers at least in part because of their simplicity and the ease with which they can be adopted. Others, such as RAT (replacement, amplification, transformation) and TPACK (technological, pedagogical, content knowledge) are favored more by educational researchers than practitioners. All seek to provide frameworks for conceptualizing the purpose of and processes for integrating technology into teaching and learning; a perspective they share is that the function of technology in learning should be to facilitate or amplify it.

The International Society for Technology in Education (ISTE) has developed standards for students, teachers, and leaders. These sets of standards describe effective practice without espousing the implementation of any specific strategy or product. Make no mistake though, for many teachers the integration of technology into teaching and learning is a daunting task because it requires a unique way of thinking.

In contrast, the incorporation of a new strategy for, say, group discussion is additive: it is like replacing a part (of the learning process) with a similar part. The implementation of instructional and digital technologies is often much more disruptive—to the teacher's thinking and habits, to the routines of a class, and to student's learning outcomes. These can all be very positive effects. But in the context of massively complex work, a willingness to embrace disruptive change is intimidating.

While we are here, let's notice categories of instructional technologies. Far from a recommendation of specific products, this is meant to spotlight the fact of the great complexity of this *part* of the practice of implementing effective strategies.

- Tools to make the processes of learning work better or more efficiently. These programs or devices enhance teaching and learning practices that were happening anyway.
  - Learning management systems create entire virtual classrooms with spaces for posting assignments, group discussions, submitting assignments, built-in feedback tools, and a range of additional tools, depending on the specific product
  - Widgets for randomizing who gets called on next
  - Video and digital content created by textbook/instructional resource providers in alignment with, and to enhance, their analog content
  - Tools for creating multimedia presentations
  - Digital review/quizzing applications

- Tools to streamline or enhance the tasks required to operate a classroom.
  - Digital attendance taking
  - Electronic grade books and grade reporting systems
  - Communication tools (between groups of teachers, teachers and students, teachers and parents)—email, blogs and websites, group communication applications, etc.
- Tools that use some level of artificial intelligence to evaluate student learning and/or deliver "individualized" lessons in specific content areas for them to complete.

IN ACTION

If you have ever been tempted to think of PE instructors as a different level or class of teacher, you need to visit Mr. Ma Suy's classes. Far from being free time or simply play period for students, his Physical Education classes place just as much emphasis on the "education" as they do on the "physical"—sometimes more. Here are some of the strategies you will see when you visit Mr. Ma Suy's classes.

As a middle school PE teacher, Mr. Ma Suy knows that routines are important for students. At the beginning of each class, students have "community time." A different student leads stretching and "good things"—an opportunity for students to share something good. Through modeling, Mr. Ma Suy has influenced students to share little tidbits of something good that has recently happened in their life that usually connects to the concepts they are studying.

The overall focus of the PE program is on healthy living and exploration. In particular, students learn about and explore sports they have probably never heard of, let alone participated in: field hockey, badminton, square dancing, soccer, stickball, tennis, ultimate Frisbee, lacrosse, and lots more.

The specific strategy that Mr. Ma Suy uses to practice sports is a type of cooperative grouping. Students are assigned to a group of four or five (groups are shuffled every few days). During part of the lesson, each group visits stations where they practice the skills specific to one sport. One student in each group is assigned to be a coach, providing feedback on form and technique. By rotating roles and groups, all students are invested in both their learning and the learning of others.

A major part of Mr. Ma Suy's physical education class is research. Students look for information about the sports and the healthy living principle they are studying. Mr. Ma Suy partners with the "core" teachers to ensure that the research and communication strategies he teaches reinforce what students are learning in their other subjects. Occasionally the group uses a portion of the period for this work but they often have homework! By assigning each student a different piece of a larger learning task, Mr. Ma Suy ensures that they work together to build their understanding.

Thanks to his grant-writing skills, Mr. Ma Suy has secured funding and purchased an impressive set of equipment and tools for his students' learning. In addition to the equipment for the nonstandard sports the students play, technology plays a big role in the program. They have GoPro cameras that they use to record and analyze data (like events in their track and field unit), a set of step-tracking bracelets that the class uses to analyze their activity for a week each semester, and a class blog for which students write entries about their learning.

An activity that Mr. Ma Suy requires regularly from his students is a reflection on their learning. He often assigns students in pairs at the end of class to respond to a prompt. For example "Based on your experience today, is it more important to be fast or strong in lacrosse. Explain." He requires student blog entries to focus on this type of reflection on learning.

As we discussed earlier in the chapter, it is nearly impossible to name all the possible strategies a teacher might use for instruction. Indeed a teacher's ability to adapt a strategy to a particular subject area, context, and age group adds to that volume of options. The key idea is that implementing effective strategies hinges on the teacher's ability to skillfully select strategies well matched to the learning target and what he knows of the students. Randomly selected and mandated strategies obviously can be implemented. Maximal impact, however, depends on the process of purposefully selecting the best possible option.

IMPLICATIONS?

This section serves as an excellent microcosm of teaching in that it is vast in its complexity. It is entirely possible as a teacher to spend an entire career implementing instructional strategies from just one of the areas we have explored—project-based teaching, for example. There are so many objectively effective strategies to select from that determining which is best in a given instructional situation can be daunting.

But if you are tempted to retort "so just pick one" or "why does it even matter," you may be missing the critical nature of this part of teaching. As we observed in the last chapter, students must engage in their learning; *what* they do to engage has a direct impact on how effective the learning is.

Teachers: stay focused on what approaches to teaching and learning best serve the ultimate goal of student learning. Make decisions based on that every time. In general, technological tools provide the opportunity to amplify your practice and your students' learning and are worth including in your decision-making process. The implementation of a technological or digital strategy or tool should lighten your work load (and/or the students') or enhance your students' learning. Or both. Beware of "shiny object syndrome" though; the goal is more student learning, never making a splash.

Two admonitions for **administrators** in this chapter: dictating to an entire school or district *which* instructional strategies they should use is a communication of how little you trust the professional judgment of your teachers. Yes, doing so makes it easier for you to "inspect what you expect." But there is little evidence that requiring a large group of professionals to take the same approach to incredibly complex work does anything more than narrow their focus. Turn your attention instead to developing the expertise of each teacher on your team and developing their ability to match instructional strategies to the learning goals and the needs of the students.

The second point is like the first. Technology holds no magic; do not hang your hat on any one product or approach. Technological tools are like textbooks or math manipulatives or the lab supplies you purchase. Of course they are powerful tools for learning, but they are not more important to student learning than a teacher. It is too easy and too common to send the message that the tool is the thing. Be aware and be careful.

Faculty: remember that you cannot teach preservice teachers all the things they will need to know in the time they are with you. And remember that the very timely examples you use today are likely to be obsolete in five or ten years. Focus on *how* a teacher makes decisions about which instructional strategies to implement, instead of on what those decisions should be.

Preservice teachers: learn all you can now and plug into a network of educators to support your continued learning as you begin your career. There is too much to know about what works when and under which circumstances. On-the-job learning is appropriate and far more powerful than the (appropriate and necessary) approach of essentially hypothetical learning you are experiencing now. Build an arsenal of knowledge but also build a commitment to continue learning. The best teachers grow their expertise—and adjust their practice—every year.

Policy-makers: avoid hyper-specific mandates. Teaching is too complicated, too messy to require specific practice universally. Instead, promote standards of practice and build structures that support the development of the capacity required for expert decision-making.

WHERE DOES THIS FIT IN TEACHING?

Implementing effective strategies is at the heart of teaching. It is an essential part of the act of teaching. We have framed this as action the teacher takes in the context of a lesson but all strategies for instruction assume the active involvement of students. Implementing effective instructional strategies, might be viewed as the ying to the yang of student engagement. From another perspective, someone who has missed or who rejects the complexity of teaching could offer this as teaching itself—the things a teacher does to cause learning to occur.

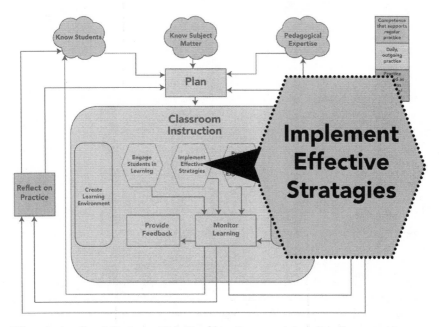

Where Instructional Strategies Fit in Teaching. *Source: original digitally created image.*

Because teaching addresses so vast a range of subject matter, such a variety of learners, and occurs in such different contexts, "effective strategies" is not and cannot be singular. To do this work adequately well requires an understanding of the students, and an understanding of the subject matter, an understanding of how learning works, the resources available, and the making of skillful decisions that synthesize those factors—and a host of others. This accessing of disparate sets of information to make the best possible decision about how to guide student learning *is* teaching.

Chapter 8

Provide Authentic
Learning Experiences

*Designing and implementing learning activities
that are meaningful and relevant to students*

*Authentic learning experiences mean you give the students multiple ways to
receive the information;* meaningful *ways to receive the information. Don't give
them busy work; don't give them assignments that are absolutely meaningless
just because you have to fill your grade book. You provide learning experiences
that are actually important not just for "meeting standards," but for their own
growth.* (Amber Emerson, middle school science teacher)

Provide Authentic Learning Experiences. *Source: original digitally created image.*

The research emphasizes the importance of learning that goes beyond knowledge acquisition and is relevant to students immediately and as a basis for future learning and action.

In the same way that it is possible to argue that there are major pieces of teaching that are not treated as such in this exploration (such as instructional technology as discussed in the last chapter), it is also possible to argue that the subject of this chapter is better suited as a subsection and not its own practice. Indeed, these three chapters that we are viewing as the heart of the act of teaching could be viewed as a single, massive piece. Based on the attention given to the importance of providing authentic learning experiences in the research literature, however, and the growing prioritization of it in practice, we will examine it separately.

As we discussed in chapter 6, these practices are intertwined and overlapping. Students should be engaged in authentic learning experiences. Teachers should prioritize strategies that aim to provide authentic learning experiences. But each area of practice is broader than the points of overlap so it is worth our while to notice authentic learning experiences as integral to the act of teaching in its own right. Think of it as the *how* and the *why* of the act of teaching.

PROVIDE AUTHENTIC LEARNING EXPERIENCES

The third subset of professional competencies and practices that describes instructional practice is providing students with purposeful, worthwhile, meaningful learning experiences. Teachers must integrate real-world learning activities by providing students with authentic problems and field-based learning experiences. This can look like students seeing how experts solve problems and subsequently experiencing expert-like investigations by using what they know to explore, create, and construct solutions.

This part of teaching can sometimes be de-emphasized as unnecessary. The thinking goes something like *students do not need to have real experiences using math to solve problems, they just need to do math.* Or *it's too dangerous to let students create chemical reactions, they can read about them or watch videos.* This line of thinking tends to forget that the purpose of learning is doing. While learning is inherently valuable in the abstract, learning a specific thing is not valuable unless the learning is actionable in some way.

It is also important to remember that the process of learning simply works better when the learner perceives it as more real and valuable. Creating authenticity in learning experiences, then, is not a matter seeking to entertain students but a means of increasing the efficacy of the learning itself.

WHAT DOES THE RESEARCH SAY?

Authentic problem-posing is recommended in teaching and learning as a means of teaching students 21st-century skills. To engage in approaches to learning like this, students need to leave their school and use their city or community as a classroom. Such interactions can provide the catalyst for providing students opportunities for civic engagement. Authentic learning requires that students consider issues from a variety of vantage points and discuss controversial issues. Whether in the learning laboratory environment of their classroom or actively engaged in their community, students learn more deeply when their learning is real and relevant.

All students learn more deeply when they engage in authentic experiences. Teachers should design and provide these experiences for *all* students, including those who receive special education services and who are behind in terms of grade-level learning goals, instead of only to students classified as gifted or accelerated in their learning.

FOR EXAMPLE?

The premise underlying this practice is that learning has far more meaning to students and sparks greater levels of mastery when the process of learning includes real, relevant content and contexts. This perspective is at least partially in response to the drift of education toward a wholly theoretical or hypothetical approach.

For example, students are made to learn to solve mathematical problems without grasping the theory of mathematical thinking or even its purpose. Right answers are often valued over meaningful understanding. Authentic learning calls for learning to move beyond the mere acquisition of cold facts or procedures of a subject area to be explicitly positioned in the context of an issue or situation relevant to the students personally or (at least) within a context where the skill or subject matter has meaning.

The construct of providing authentic learning experiences is meant to apply to all subject areas at all levels. What follows is a brief list of examples of what authentic learning could look like for students in a variety of subjects and settings.

Approaches to authentic learning:

- Project-based learning. This approach uses the structure of a project to organize authentic learning about a topic. Students conduct research, build knowledge and understanding, and create a product or presentation to demonstrate their learning. Student voice in the learning process provides the opportunity to develop authenticity. When implemented skillfully, project-based learning ensures that students have a great deal of control over the activities they engage in but are also required to align those activities with the learning goals.

- Problem-based learning. Students select a real issue or problem that impacts them or their community in some way, conduct research on the problem, and develop evidence-based, real recommendations for addressing those issues. The teacher arranges the process to ensure that students' research and study addresses content-area standards. Providing genuine purpose to the study makes the learning authentic for students. Whenever possible, students actually propose their solutions to decision-makers for consideration.
- Case-based learning. Similar to project- and problem-based learning, case-based learning presents students with scenarios that are typical of or similar to real-world examples. This approach may be preferred when it is necessary or prudent to use models that are realistic but more hypothetical than problem-based learning seeks to be.
- Internships, job shadowing. For some subjects and skills, students can learn in the specific context where those skills and content are used in the real world. While such placements have general benefits to students as learning experiences, the impact can be amplified by purposeful alignment of the course's learning goals and the actual experience itself. While placements of this type are more common at the secondary level, brief experiences—such as a single day shadowing a professional—can have great value to the learning of students as young as elementary school.

Examples of authentic learning:

- Develop solutions for packing lunches equitably with an odd number of items (i.e., seven sandwiches for four people)
- Identify causes of traffic congestion at the intersections near the school and recommend solutions to the city
- Research and recommend three new sports/activities to add to PE
- Suggest strategies for addressing blood bank shortages during certain parts of the year
- Create a plan to reduce the amount of recess time taken up waiting for classes to transition to/from the playground
- Propose municipal solutions to the problem of invasive plant species
- Draft alternate bell schedules to improve delays during lunch periods
- Research and present recommendations to the city council for strategies to encourage citizens to shop local

- Identify reasons why student attendance at athletic events is low and suggest strategies for increasing participation to the athletic director and school principal

IN ACTION

Mr. Able considers his art class an important part of his student's development as thinkers and members of their community. Throughout the year, his students study and work in a variety of artistic mediums. An important part of their learning is also using their art to impact the world around them. By the end of every year, each student is required to produce at least one work designed to address or call attention to an issue in the school or the community. Each year, his students work together to choose a different approach to this challenge. Ideas have included

- Designing a logo for a local nonprofit
- Creating a mural for a public space
- Creating designs for public service announcement billboards
- Choosing a theme for the school art show and creating individual pieces
- Creating "junk art" from items found in a public park as a way of highlighting the importance of caring for shared spaces

For Mr. Able it is important for his students to find purpose in their art. For many, art is an outlet of self-expression. For some, it is about exploration and learning. No matter what though, art should be real and meaningful. For some students their best work is *not* produced as part of the local issue challenge— perhaps because the issue does not impact them personally. But for most students, the process that Mr. Able uses helps them to think of their work as producing art instead of as completing assignments—and that is at least in part because they work to give their art meaning beyond the classroom.

IMPLICATIONS?

Teachers: keep it real. The *best* question a student can ask you is "when will I use this?" When learning has meaning, students will engage more deeply and make more meaningful progress toward mastery. Admittedly, there may be instructional standards or content details for which that question is difficult to answer. Take the time to dig in and find that answer. In regard to incorporating authentic learning experiences, aim (at the least) to incorporate case-based examples in your classroom. That is, build the learning around considering issues that are realistic and meaningful to students.

Whenever possible, present students with *actual* issues that exist in your community and are connected to learning goals. That approach can provide the structure for meaningful cross-curricular learning as most problems are not one-dimensional and can provide the opportunity for deep learning across a number of subject areas.

Preservice teachers: collect ideas, pay attention to the local news, and develop the habit of asking yourself "how could addressing that issue provide students the context for meaningful learning?" Keep in mind that the topic that is very important to a community today is unlikely to remain so for several years; the best problem-based learning plans have a finite life-expectancy before they lose their relevance to students. It is not the development of detailed plans that will be valuable to you but the development of the ability to see opportunities to enhance learning around you all the time.

Administrators: the implementation of authentic learning depends most heavily on the teachers in your school; they must be empowered to make decisions. The authors of textbooks do not live in your community; while they can suggest ideas, following their recommendations "to fidelity" is likely to diminish the benefits of authentic learning experiences for your students. Designing and implementing authentic learning takes time; create space in your school's schedule to plan well.

Give a team of teachers a day to plan, clear space in the schedule for high-impact collaborative work, say yes when your teachers point outside the box. The profession considers the providing of authentic learning experiences integral to the very nature of teaching. It is your responsibility to create the structures and supports that make it possible for those expectations to be enacted well by the teachers in your team.

WHERE DOES THIS FIT IN TEACHING?

The notion this book is built on is that teaching is more complex than is generally realized or acknowledged—even within education. Indeed, if it were not so, the book could be much shorter, highlighting the few essential pieces to teaching. Even in such a shorter discussion of the obvious parts of teaching, the importance of authentic learning would be made plain. Learning must have meaning. Education does not have value if it is completely abstract—indeed its value grows as it develops knowledge and habits upon which future action can be built.

Authentic learning experiences, then, are the third pillar of the heart of the act of teaching. Teaching *engages* students in the learning process. Teaching leverages *strategies* specifically designed to maximize progress toward the learning goal(s). And teaching simply works better and the learning takes deeper root when it is *authentic* and *meaningful* to students.

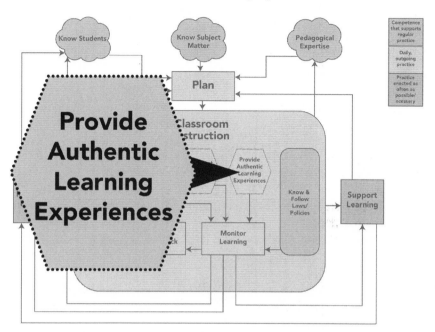

Where the Implementation of Effective Strategies Fits in Teaching. *Source: original digitally created image.*

Another term often used to describe the importance of this component of teaching is "relevance." Subject matter that is made relevant to a student is mastered more deeply. The mandate to learn is not inherently motivating to students. "Because you have to," "because it's on the test," and "because it's a standard" may all be factually correct answers to the quintessential student question "why are we learning this?" but they do nothing to make learning relevant to students.

Not only is the question fair, it is also essential. The most powerful answer to the question is learning experiences that are explicitly relevant and meaningful to the student. In this way, learning becomes real and authentic.

Chapter 9

Support Learning

Identifying and providing a wide range of supports to advance student learning

It is not enough to lob information at students. Sometimes I hear people say "I taught it, they just didn't learn it." For me, if the students didn't learn it that means I said it but I didn't teach it. Teaching includes noticing when students are not learning and adding supports, continuing the process or even starting over. (Chris Tomkins, immersion teacher)

Support Learning. *Source: original digitally created image.*

Teaching is not merely the passive dispensing of knowledge but requires teachers to design and/or implement structures to ensure that *all* students learn.

In this chapter we turn our attention to practice that has not traditionally been part of teaching. For a long time, the teacher was cast as the dispenser of knowledge, the setter of tasks, and the judge of academic attainment. The responsibility for learning fell entirely on the student. If he/she did not understand, he/she had better find someone to help him/her improve his/her understanding. If he/she needed more time, he/she was well advised to stay awake as long as it took. If learning did not occur, it was the fault and the responsibility of the student.

That view of teaching and learning has shifted steadily over the last several decades due to a number of influencing factors, not least of which has been the national dialogue on the "crisis" in education and the actual impact of "accountability" measures in schools.

To be sure, educational outcomes in the American educational system continue to be in want of improvement. There is no question of whether every student deserves a high-quality education. The responsibility for ensuring more desirable outcomes falls largely to classroom teachers. By definition now, teaching includes the identifying and the mitigation of factors that threaten students' learning.

SUPPORT LEARNING

Teaching includes identifying and providing a wide range of supports to advance student learning. The picture of teaching painted by the professional literature is far different from the paradigm of teacher as dispenser of knowledge. The research calls for teachers to be flexible and responsive to student needs. Key to this approach is for the teacher to support learning through differentiated instruction; implementation of interventions and supports tailored to individual student need; and adjustment, repetition, and sustaining of interventions to the extent necessary to ensure success.

WHAT DOES THE RESEARCH SAY?

The research makes clear that "one size fits all" teaching is insufficient to ensure positive learning outcomes for all students. Teachers should use differentiated instruction as a method of providing different ways to acquire knowledge, process information, and create different products so that each student can learn in the way that is most productive for him/her.

This means, in part, that the teacher needs to tailor instruction to the level of learner expertise as it changes during learning. To that end, the teacher provides tailored instructional guidance and adjusts learning tasks to meet students' needs based on their engagement in and performance on tasks.

Schools and school districts design curriculum that expands upon students' *actual* rather than assumed misunderstandings. Standardized test scores tend to make everyone look alike, when in fact instruction in school should be developing unique talents. The most challenging work for students is to craft individual solutions rather than finding a common answer the teacher expects. Learning goals should be appropriately challenging, and supported by materials, methods, and assessments that are diverse, flexible, and responsive to the learning needs and opportunities of students.

Individualized and differentiated instruction requires that the teacher monitor their students' understanding, and then look for opportunities to specifically support individual students' growth toward the learning goal. Adjustments should be made for students who are already below grade level. Some adjustments are accommodations (alterations that provide accessibility), while others are modifications (changes in form or degree of difficulty).

One specific approach to skillfully supporting student learning is referred to as scaffolding. Scaffolding is a practice in which the teacher "temporarily takes over parts of student tasks with the goal of transferring the responsibility for the task back to the student at a later point in time" (van de Pol, Volman, & Beishuizen, 2011, p. 46).

In the support of learning, teachers enact peer tutoring, tutor and reteach students themselves, and provide enrichment activities for students who demonstrate mastery level learning more quickly than their peers. Teachers also identify and address students' emotional needs. In order to be able to support learning more effectively, teachers consider and mitigate non-academic factors that may stand in the way of student learning such as the effects of poverty, physical or cognitive disability, and students' emotional health.

FOR EXAMPLE?

Let us tread carefully here in our exploration of teaching. This practice is at the same time integral to teaching (as it should be) and beyond the scope of what teaching has been and may be in the minds of some not directly involved with teaching. It is difficult to exaggerate the degree of complexity and difficulty this dimension of teaching introduces to the job. A lecturer is a teacher. But—in the K–12 setting at least—the dissemination of information typical of lecture (however engaging it might be) would be considered wholly incomplete and unsatisfactory teaching. A lecture is not designed to bend, flex, and adapt based on the emergent needs of the learners.

A better metaphor for teaching is that of a master guiding an apprentice; observing his/her work, providing feedback, repeating lessons, or seeking new ways to teach a difficult concept. The nurturing of deep learning for the individual. For every student. Simultaneously. The complexity of teaching is not the near impossibility of any single part of the work, it is the intricacy and variability of almost all the parts of the work and the sheer volume and pace of the work.

Supporting student learning is now a base expectation of teaching but is also not singular. A few examples of what this practice can look like follows.

- Elementary small groups. Standard practice in elementary grade classrooms (and sometimes used at other grade spans) is structured small group instruction—typically five students or fewer. The teacher groups students based on the evidence of their learning progress on the specific skill or content the class is studying. Instruction is customized to fit the learning needs of the students.
- Providing student choice is a form of individualization. Teachers design a number of learning tasks that are substantively different but that all address the same learning target and invite students to choose their path to learning. By flexing assignments to address varying student interests, modes of production, or other design factors, teachers ensure that learning is the goal, not completion of specific assignments.
- As a variation of the last concept, learning "stations" are excellent opportunities for differentiation in the classroom. Stations provide multiple ways of attacking the same learning objectives through autonomous or semi-autonomous work. Students either rotate through each station or are allowed to choose one or more stations.
- Technology-assisted individualization is increasingly prevalent and popular. A wide range of educational technology products seek to streamline and automate the process of providing students individualized lessons in one or more subject areas. The products typically use either teacher selection or built-in pretests to identify lessons for students to engage in.
- One-on-one teaching is still an important part of the range of services used to support student learning. For the typical teacher with a full teaching schedule, tutoring or "intervention," as it is sometimes called, must occur outside the normal schedule—before/after school, during lunch or recess,

or at a similar part of the day. Some schools are able to make room in teachers' schedules to dedicate to individualized instruction or even hire teachers who specialize in individual or small-group instruction.
- Similar to the process required for providing students choice, teachers may modify or "level" an assignment based on student learning needs.
- Student learning can involve adjustments to the environment in which the learning takes place. Arrangements can be made for students with tactile or sensory sensitivities to complete specific tasks or assessments in a place that is less distracting for them. Changes can be made to the classroom that would be essentially unnoticed by most students but beneficial to one or more—such as work to change the lighting in a room
- Teachers can make procedural changes to their practice to support student learning. For example, they can adjust their grading practices to allow students the opportunity to continue their learning after the first attempt and reassess when they have in fact extended their learning.

These are just a handful of the approaches teachers take to support their students' learning. What these practices have in common is the philosophical position that the responsibility for learning is shared by the teacher and the student. While the student does bear responsibility for engaging in the process of learning, he is not responsible for removing all the barriers to that learning alone.

IN ACTION

Ms. Flores, a National Board Certified high school math teacher, considers differentiated instruction the most important part of her work as a teacher. She speaks often about the importance of "diagnosing" individual student's learning and "prescribing" learning matched exactly to their need. If you were to spend a day in Ms. Flores's class, there is an excellent chance it would look something like this.

In each class, Ms. Flores begins with a discussion of the assessment the students took earlier in the week. She has marked each error the students made on the quiz but did not include any notes or a grade. Student seats are arranged in groups of four and as Ms. Flores returns the quizzes, the groups begin *discussing* the quiz: What's the mistake here? Oh look, I divided instead of multiplying. I think you missed a step on that question.

After the group discussions, the students each spend a few minutes identifying the errors they made on the quiz. The same error three times is one error; three different errors on the same question is three errors. As the activity closes, Ms. Flores collects the quizzes.

Your opportunity to continue your learning journey starts now. The grades for this quiz will post tonight but I want to see who is willing to put the work in to move at least a little bit closer to mastering this!

Next, the classes are introduced to a "math meal." They had noticed the apron Ms. Flores was wearing when they entered the room and now she takes out tri-folded sheets of paper that look like restaurant menus. Inside they see the plan for today's learning: everyone must pick two of the five "appetizer" activities, one of the two "main course" activities, and one of the three "desert" activities. All the activities are tied to the concept they are tackling in this unit: solving inequalities. All the resources students need to complete the activities they select are stationed around the room.

Ms. Flores checks in with each student, discussing their "order" with them and answering questions. "Yes, you do have to complete the appetizers first. No, you can't do just the deserts, that's not a healthy math meal." She knows that the activities in each activity are different ways of pursuing the same learning. This approach is designed to give students autonomy and choice while ensuring that their choices move their learning in the right direction.

After students have started on their "meal," Ms. Flores begins inviting students to "put our heads together." Using the patterns of errors she had observed on the quiz (but had not written for the students to see), she does quick mini-lessons with students. They review concepts, talk about their misunderstandings, and identify what they need to do next. Her students have gotten comfortable with talking about their learning and are used to hearing their classmates talk about "what's next" and do so themselves. Sometimes these discussions include two or three students sitting next to each other who are struggling with the same concepts but often it is a one-on-one conversation.

In a few cases, Ms. Flores invites the student to come back for "lunch and learn" the next day so they can have more time to tackle the issue. Each conversation is based on the evidence of that student's learning; the assignment each student has (their own personal "what's next") is designed to connect their current understanding with the learning goal.

IMPLICATIONS?

Policy-makers: seek out opportunities to visit schools and (specifically) to see what supporting student learning looks like in action. In case you are not aware, schools and teachers feel pressured to put their very best foot forward when you are in the building. For this reason (and others), it is likely that your understanding of this part of teaching is incomplete. Here's a specific idea: make arrangements to work or volunteer as a *tutor* or an interventionist in a school. Go somewhere where the teachers and students will not know your name. Be there as a student of teaching, not as an observer of the state of the school in particular or education in general.

The parts of teaching we have discussed so far are very complicated and require a great deal of both skill and labor. Identifying the interferences to the learning of individual students and diagnosing the appropriate interventions is arguably more difficult and certainly more time-consuming. When you do visit, spend the whole day. Teachers return to the work every day—immersing yourself for six hours is exponentially better than a visit that lasts just one or two hours.

Teachers: you know the importance of differentiated and individualized instruction. And you know how unspeakably heavy that lift is. Don't do it alone. Join networks of educators—in your building, your district, around the country. The job (and this part of the job in particular) is literally impossible to do alone. Help lift the load of others by sharing ideas and examples and templates and receive their support in return.

Administrators: resist the temptation to seek overly simplistic solutions to advance student learning. Technology-based tools have their place but can do more harm than good (in terms of real, sustainable student learning) when they are treated as silver bullets. Work to build structures and systems that strengthen the hands of teachers as they do this work. It is also critically important that you not let the weight of responsibility for student learning rest mostly on teachers. You are right to set high expectations for educators. Hold students to high expectations as well. And make sure that you shoulder at least as much responsibility as the others in your organization.

Faculty: seek ways to prepare preservice teachers for this part of teaching. As performance-based assessment (such as edPTA) becomes more widely required for graduation from colleges of education, look to the teacher assessments upon which it was modeled (such as National Board Certification) for frameworks of developing emergent skills toward accomplished practice. At the heart of these initiatives is using available information about student learning to make decisions to support their learning. Entering the workforce with the groundwork for that mode of thinking firmly laid will serve your students well.

WHERE DOES THIS FIT IN TEACHING?

Supporting student learning is equally likely to be a part of teaching taken as a matter of course and to be surprising. The parts of teaching explored to this point are vital to the process and the act of teaching. Supporting student learning is just as critical to the nature of teaching. In fact, in many ways, it is not separate from many other parts. Student supports must be planned. These supports work best when they are engaging for students. And providing authentic learning experiences is supportive of learning. This part of teaching refers to actions that are deeply embedded into whole-group instruction or the lesson—the base, standard, normal part of a class. But it also refers to *additional* actions taken for, with, or by specific students.

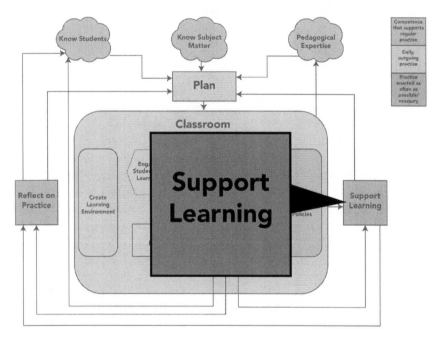

Where Supporting Learning Fits in Teaching. *Source: original digitally created image.*

There is no leeway for a teacher to choose to teach the whole class *or* focus instruction on small groups or individual students. Teaching encompasses both: instruction that is guided by advancement toward learning standards established at the state level *and* instruction continuously modulated to meet individual students at the point of their current learning. If this expectation sounds unreasonable or impossible, perhaps it provides a small glimpse into the reality of teaching for millions of teachers.

Chapter 10

Monitor Learning

Actively and continuously monitoring the degree to which students are learning

My plan is to always set expectations and help students meet them. Now some of my students will tell you that I'm hard and I'm tough. In their lingo, I am always "doing too much." But I treat them like scholars. I give them a scholar's path and help keep them on the path. (Dr. Lisa Stewart, high school ELA teacher)

Monitor Learning. *Source: original digitally created image.*

Monitoring includes creating structures and practices that seek evidence of student learning. The activities students engage in are opportunities to learn *and* for the teacher to observe and collect evidence of that learning.

Evaluation is an important part of *all* processes intended to make, produce, or nurture something. The heat and temper of a metal must be closely

83

monitored throughout the manufacturing process to ensure that the final product meets the required specifications. The growth of each plant in an entire field or greenhouse must be continuously observed to ensure that the plant itself and its produce are within the desirable parameters. Incremental development of specific skills by athletes is tracked in order to ensure progress toward performance goals.

Unless any outcome will do, it is essential to keep track of where the current performance is in relationship to the goal. The entire academic purpose of teaching is to advance all students to learning goals. Monitoring the state of progress toward those goals is integral to teaching itself.

MONITOR LEARNING

Teaching includes actively and continuously monitoring the degree to which students are learning. Effective teaching includes active monitoring of student learning for the purpose of understanding how each student's attainment or understanding compares to specific goals for learning. Over the last two or three decades, hyper-attention to standardized forms of assessment—a legitimate and important part of the puzzle, particularly for *groups* of students (classrooms, schools, districts, etc.)—has ironically caused a narrowing of focus on that *form* of assessment as what matters. In too many cases, "accountability" is really about raising test scores rather than improving actual student learning outcomes.

Perhaps that trend is entirely predictable when instruments designed to provide an *overview* of progress in a narrow band of practice become the grounds for drawing sweeping conclusions about schools and districts. The cases for and against standardized testing in general and the role it plays in public education are complex and abundant enough to provide fodder for deep discussion but are beyond the scope of this exploration of teaching. The relevant point is that monitoring student learning is far more complicated and nuanced than the administration of big tests a few times each year. The teacher must monitor and manage student work and learning frequently and as a natural part of the classroom culture.

WHAT DOES THE RESEARCH SAY?

To enact this type of monitoring of student learning, a teacher must hold a strong understanding of the nature of assessment: both assessment of learning and assessment that drives learning. That foundation allows the use of an objective accountability system based on observable, measurable evidence of learning. Criteria of assessment are shared with students to make clear what evidence will best reflect the achievement of learning goals.

Monitoring student learning is a complex and perpetual practice for the effective teacher. By developing and conducting multiple forms of assessment, teachers are able to collect and analyze meaningful data about student learning. Formative assessments, rubrics, achievement-based assessments, work samples and productions, questioning, student self-assessment, and performances of real-world skills are all valid approaches to monitoring student learning. Instead of labeling unsuccessful attempts as failures, teachers view errors as opportunities for learning and interpret the information they gain from student errors as a source of guidance for future instruction.

FOR EXAMPLE?

Do not think of this domain of teaching as *assessment* or even *evaluation*. Both are part of the larger body of practice built around monitoring the learning of students. These terms are often used as significantly overlapping or even interchangeable but both terms (as they are typically used in practice) include only a portion of the work a teacher must do to monitor student learning. For the sake of clearly seeing the scope of monitoring learning as it exists in teaching, consider these examples.

Examination—monitoring learning includes enacting one or more (typically many more) forms of testing a student's knowledge. Although they are essentially identical in nature, "tests" are typically conceived as more important or significant than "quizzes," perhaps because the former are usually designed to include more questions than the latter and to carry more weight or points. Both are used as formal mechanisms for evaluating individual students' learning. Formal examinations of learning may include (but are certainly not limited to)

- Multiple-choice items
- Questions requiring a short, written answer
- More open-ended questions requiring a more extensive answer (i.e., essay questions)
- Fact-/knowledge-based questions—matching, fill-in-the-blank, etc.

Observing and/or collecting evidence—a teacher also monitors student learning through observation and collection (formally or informally) of evidence of the student's knowledge and understanding. While teaching certainly does include the act of imparting, dispensing, guiding to, and otherwise presenting content and skills to students, it also includes a continuous professional *noticing* of how well that learning is being absorbed or internalized by students.

While public education's current climate tends to frame standardized and formalized measurements of student learning as superior or more reliable, both teaching and learning depend on the continuous monitoring of the current state of (learning) affairs in order to stay on track. A list of ways in which a teacher can observe and collect evidence would be longer than the whole of this book. Just a few examples are as follows:

- Asking questions—perhaps one of the most deceptively complex and nuanced parts of teaching. Effective questioning is not easily mastered.
- Student work samples—artifacts produced by students can serve as evidence of their understanding of specific standards or learning targets.
- Student performance—mastery can be displayed through observable action. Counting to twenty, playing a piece of music, speaking a (second) language, etc.

Benchmarking and triangulation—the observation and documentation of data points have no inherent value to student learning. It is the process of interpreting and making sense of such evidence that brings value to both the learner for his/her learning and the teacher for his/her teaching. Twin components are integral. Effective evaluation of student learning requires a benchmark from which to work. Content standards for learning provide the foundation for such an understanding but the process works most effectively when teachers and students share an understanding of what the standard means and what mastery can or would look like.

In other words, it must be clear what students should know and be able to do. *Then* what a student actually knows and is actually able to do can be compared to that standard. The purpose of such comparisons should be both evaluative ("this is the student's attainment") and formative ("because the learning has X relationship to the standard, Y additional learning is required to match the standard"). Key to this work is the identification of multiple pieces of evidence of student learning. Single data points can be misleading—even when they are accurate. Effective practice seeks a body of evidence of students' learning and values a range of modes of evidence.

IN ACTION

Never try to stump Ms. Bowling about where her 3rd graders stand in regard to their learning; she always knows. She figured out some time ago that the key to a successful classroom is having an accurate understanding of each student's learning. If you know what to look for, you would notice that she embeds a search for information about her students' learning into every part of the day.

Each morning, Ms. Bowling greets her students at the door. As they enter, she notices which color they tap on a small, four-color poster outside the door. The whole class has talked many times about recognizing and naming their own emotions. The students signal roughly which "zone of regulation" they are in. Ms. Bowling knows that, for eight- and nine-year-olds especially, *any* emotion interplays with the learning process. Being excited, sad, angry, frustrated, silly, tired, or feeling dozens of other emotions makes a difference for learning. So she begins her day with these little clues of how to customize the way she interacts with each student.

At the start of every class, students participate in morning meetings. Among the routines they have established as a class is "My Nut to Crack." Each student tries to articulate one challenge or specific learning goal he or she wants to meet that day. Students have learned to reflect on their own learning and think about what they need to tackle next. Sharing one goal for the day helps them focus their work and tips off Ms. Bowling to how to support them.

The strategy that would probably stand out to a visitor most dramatically is the number of questions Ms. Bowling asks students. This is a skill she has worked to hone. She has created a strategy for keeping track of who she asks questions to and works to ask every student at least one question every hour—more if possible.

She uses questions strategically, occasionally asking students a question they know the answer to as a boost to their confidence but more often asking questions that take some thought. Her questions are usually not addressed to the entire class—so students do not compete with each other to answer or avoid embarrassment by trying not to answer questions.

All of the 3rd grade teachers in Ms. Bowling's school work together as a highly functioning professional learning community. The work they spend the most time on together is developing strong common understanding of learning standards, agreeing on what mastery should or could look like, and designing common assessments to "ping" student learning regularly. Each teacher collects the responses or results from their students and then, as a team, they look for trends and try to make sense of what they see. Their guiding question is "what does this evidence tell us about students' learning?"

That focus translates to the student level as well; a seeking to keep an accurate read on individual progress.

When all the students in school participate in standardized assessments (usually three times each year), Ms. Bowling uses that information as a puzzle piece for understanding each child's learning. She asks how the information the assessment provides should inform the plan for learning for that student.

One more noteworthy piece of Ms. Bowling's practice is the role of her students in monitoring their own learning. Unlike the practice she knows other schools are fond of, her students do **not** know the score they made on the last standardized assessment. But they do keep close track of their current learning and how it compares to the learning target. Part of their morning routine is to *talk* about the goal for learning that day. Students are able to describe what they know and can do, what part of the learning goal they are wrestling with, and what they are doing to master that part of the target.

IMPLICATIONS?

Preservice teachers: your experiences throughout your career as a scholar are likely to have instilled in you an understanding of assessment as transactive and compensatory. It is important for you to view the entire process of monitoring learning—grading, evaluation, assessment, all of it—as wielding a flashlight and not a hammer. The purpose of monitoring learning is to notice its state and trajectory *in order to make decisions*. You have doubtless studied the concept of assessment in its many forms—summative, formative, formal, informal, etc. The purpose of collecting this information is to make informed decisions with it.

Faculty: the future teachers you are training need to understand this as a *system* of practice that is massively complex and includes the components explored above and more. Help them view this process as the collection of evidence, not merely as the tabulation of data. Most importantly, they need to understand how to make effective use of the results of this practice for decision-making.

Teachers: here are a couple of hard words for you. In spite of all the strings and pressure attached to them, standardized tests are not the most important thing. Like a tail on a pet, they have a place in teaching and learning. Also like a tail, they should not wag the dog. Consider how you view the purpose of the practices explored in this chapter. Are you like an Olympic judge looking for justification to award a summative judgment? *Nailed that element, missed that requirement; 8.5.* Or are you like a doctor? *Given these symptoms, the best action for me and for my patient is to . . . .*

The monitoring of student learning should provide you with a steady stream of evidence with which to make decisions. You know your content area and you have pedagogical expertise; monitoring student learning feeds directly (and immediately) into an ever-expanding understanding of your students. That understanding is valuable to you because it helps guide your next decisions. Your grasp of the content already told you which direction you and your students should be headed; understanding the current state of your students' learning helps you decide how best to move in that direction.

Administrators: you face incredible pressure in nearly every aspect of the job and particularly as it regards formal evaluation measures. Nevertheless, consider this simple and very hard request. Keep the focus on learning, not the symbols of learning. Resist the temptation to pursue courses of action that value the improvement of the *proxy* for learning. In the same way that it is possible to actually damage your health by focusing on lowing your blood pressure or losing weight instead of on the issues causing those problems, make it crystal clear to your team that learning itself is the goal.

Policy-makers: you can't have it both ways. You cannot expect meaningful results from a policy that sets the bar very high in specific areas without addressing the entirety of the educational system. You should expect a world-class education for our students, we all should. But demanding such results from a system missing significant pieces of the puzzle required to produce them is simply unreasonable. And to return never-endingly to the drumbeat of "improvement"—which *always* means "higher test scores" unless you explicitly and specifically name a different metric—serves to reinforce all the way down to the teacher and student level that scores are what you care about most.

WHERE DOES THIS FIT IN TEACHING?

The monitoring of learning is essential to teaching because teaching is not passive. Teaching as the dispensing of knowledge or even skill would be far less complex. But the reality is that it is not really teaching if no one is learning. And in order to determine whether and how well anyone is learning, that process must be examined. The evidence of students' learning must be compared to the goal for learning in order to be able to draw meaningful conclusions. Ultimately, this practice of monitoring is essential to accurately identify whether and how well students have learned in order to continue to advance their learning most effectively.

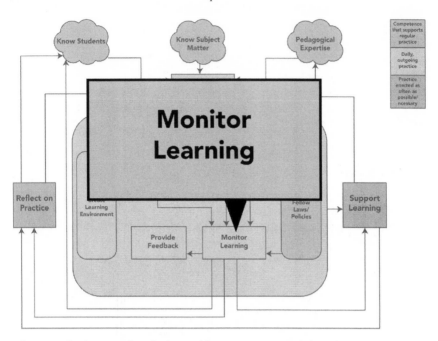

Where Monitoring Learning Fits in Teaching. *Source: original digitally created image.*

It may be helpful to think of the entire practice of monitoring learning as sonar. Sonar is used to verify a vessel's position relative to the world around it and relative to the position and trajectory it should be on. Sonar readings are devoid of judgment. They are a means of saying "you are *here*."

Contrast this with one specific use of radar—a law enforcement official's instrument. The primary function of the radar in that case is to calculate the speed at which a vehicle is traveling. If your speed is within an acceptable range you (are allowed to) pass. If your speed is *not* in the expected range, you will fail (to be free to continue on your way). Radar also documents your speed *at one moment in time*. The radar says "your speed was *wrong*." The monitoring of learning should be used the way sonar is used (to notice the current reality and to make decisions based on that reality) far more than it is used like radar (to pass summary judgment).

Chapter 11

Provide Feedback

Continuously providing specific, descriptive, individual feedback to students about their learning

If you think about it, we learn better—we learn more—when we have feedback. As a professional I crave feedback: how am I doing, what about my practice matches expectations, what needs improvement? My students need that from me too—a steady stream of feedback helps them know they are on course or make to adjustments. (AnaMaria Lopez, art teacher)

Provide Feedback. *Source: original digitally created image.*

Grades are a form of feedback but are far from adequate alone. Teaching includes ongoing dialogue about learning between teacher and students.

Feedback takes a range of forms including just-in-time comments, written descriptive feedback, marks, and more.

PROVIDE FEEDBACK

Teaching includes continuously providing specific, descriptive feedback to students about their learning—the companion practice to monitoring learning. Effective teachers use evidence of student learning as a tool for advancing that learning through substantial, constructive, and focused feedback. Feedback as we observe it here includes a broad range of actions but all are centered on parlaying the evidence of student learning (collected through the monitoring process discussed in the last chapter) into influence on learning itself.

Feedback confirms that learning is on the correct trajectory but is unfinished. Feedback identifies misconceptions *and next steps for correcting them.* Feedback describes the learning in ways that reinforce and drive it forward.

WHAT DOES THE LITERATURE SAY?

Effective teaching includes engaging in the assessment-feedback cycle frequently as long periods of performance without feedback can lead to off-target practice that yields permanence even when the concept or skill is faulty. Teachers ensure that responses to students move far beyond the traditional *Initiation, Response, Feedback* protocol and are immediate and useful, personal and salient, descriptive, open, and self-referential.

In order to ensure that feedback is maximally beneficial to student learning, teachers create a culture of trust by publicly praising student task performance and providing an endless feedback loop. However, they strive to build students' academic perseverance by providing as few explanations as possible and trying not to provide the correct answer outright. They do address students' lack of understanding, however, by offering close and supportive responses.

The professional literature calls for grades and assessment to be instruments of learning. In fact, a growing body of literature supports the conclusion that the way in which grading and assessment are implemented has a meaningful impact on student learning. In addition, assessment serves as information for planning along with the results of formative assessments. Noted author and researcher Grant Wiggins asserts that "learners need endless feedback more than they need endless teaching."

FOR EXAMPLE?

Even authors and researchers who have spent decades studying and writing about feedback say the concept is difficult to grasp well. But, for the sake of this exploration, let us notice a few of the characteristics of effective feedback—among *many*.

Immediate. Feedback is most useful to learning when it is received as soon as possible, after the antecedent action or output. A toddler cannot assimilate feedback about the inappropriateness of coloring on the wall a week after he produces his masterpiece and has forgotten about it. An athlete does not need notes about her free-thrown shooting form two days after the drill. The shorter the space between the performance and the feedback, the better that feedback is at producing learning.

Personal. While there is room for a teacher to provide feedback to entire groups of students, in general the most effective feedback is personal. Knowing that the entire class misunderstood a concept is not specifically helpful to my learning. I need to know how my performance compares to the standard and what I need to do to continue improving.

Descriptive. The purpose of feedback is not judgment—feedback is formative in nature. That is, feedback is intended to reinforce or redirect, not to label. In order to achieve that aim, feedback should be descriptive. It provides an accurate, nonjudgmental description of the performance or output. "Good job" is not feedback. *Descriptive* feedback might sound something like "The simile you used in your second paragraph—'as annoying as a hair in a biscuit'—provides a strong mental image!"

Useful. If the purpose of providing feedback is to advance learning, the feedback must be useful to the learner(s) to whom it is provided. In other words, it must be actionable. Providing an accurate description is not enough; feedback should also be provided in a way that points to relevant action for students.

It may be worth our while to briefly notice a few of the *forms* that feedback can take. While feedback can look like a lot of things, it is very common for teachers to provide feedback to students in three areas specifically: verbal feedback, written feedback, and symbolic feedback—most often grades.

Verbal feedback is a *constant* and ongoing part of teaching. If we were to look into a series of classrooms and watch student-teacher interactions for a few minutes, we would almost certainly see verbal feedback in every one. This sounds like statements of observation: "I notice that you drew the cell walls thicker on one side"; questions intended to make students reflect: "Tell me about why you chose purple for this section of the drawing"; and even simple questions designed as nudges in thinking: "Are you sure you want to divide there," "France *and* Spain? Interesting choice," and "Would a triangle fit there?"

In a way, feedback is itself an instructional strategy; this practice is often intertwined with the engagement of students in learning and implementation of effective strategies. Feedback is not something that is only done *after* learning has happened, it is part of the process.

Written feedback. The work samples that students produce provide a teacher with opportunities to provide written feedback. As we have already noted, this feedback should provide value to the student's *future* learning, not simply articulate what currently exists. Skillfully done, written feedback leverages a clear description of the current evidence of learning to suggest the best next steps for learning.

Symbolic feedback. Grading is the assigning of numbers or letters to an assignment or a collection of assignments (a "grading period" or an entire course) as a symbolic communication of student learning. Grading is argu-ably one of a very few practices that are almost universally part of teaching *and* widely, significantly misunderstood and faultily implemented. In the context of this exploration though, the relevant point is the reality that schools are expected to issue letters and/or numeric grades for students as a means of communicating how well they have learned.

Grades can be the primary mode of communicating a student's progress and attainment. In the context of monitoring student learning, that is the role they typically fill—communication. In practice, grades are often the currency of the classroom and function more as compensation than communication. "Dr. Maxey why did you *give* me a D? *I did* not *give you a D; you* earned *it!*" Whatever the quality of the practice, the issuing or assigning of grades is a significant part of teaching and is functionally tied to the process of moni-toring learning and communicating the reality of each student's attainment.

IN ACTION

It's a random day in Ms. Crutchfield's career and technical education class-room. There is welding equipment, farming equipment, power tools, hard hats, and safety goggles in sight in various parts of the classroom. But this is not your uncle's shop class. This is a thriving program with ties to industry, the local business community, and the farmers' co-op; partnerships like that don't last without maintaining very high standards of success.

This program took a lot of work to build over many years. But our observation is tuned to Ms. Crutchfield's *teaching* today and one thing stands out: a constantly running stream of feedback to students. Here are snippets of what we might hear—although probably not in a row.

> *Jamie, remind your group what the first rule of the shop is? Very good: safety first!*
>
> *Danielle and Bryan, here's what I see in your draft plan for the wreath project: the concept matches our goals for organizing a community service project and the communication is clear, catchy, and concise. Talk to me about the work schedule. I don't see details. Did I miss them?*
>
> *Okay, heroes. Let's talk about this project. The goal is to sand down and refinish these three pieces. Check out this side of the desk that Phillip did this morning. This is a great example of what it should look like when you are done sanding. I'll be back in a few minutes to check on your progress here.*
>
> *Mr. Collins and Mr. Barrett, how can I help you? Yes, the important thing to remember is that if you dig the holes too deep, the plants will not survive. This one is too low; these are all the right level. Check this section again to make sure each plant is at the right depth.*
>
> *Reflection time! What's working for us in this project? What is not working? How can we adjust to improve* [the issues identified by the students]*?*
>
> *Can I just say how impressed I am by this weld Derrick! Hold on a minute. Here's a weld you did last week. Can you look at these two welds and tell me how they are different?*
>
> *Good morning Dr. Jones. Felicia and I were just having a conversation about how well our standard fits with what you were saying on the intercom just now about being a responsible part of a community. The standard is about the importance of natural resources to the local, county and state economy. Felicia, I'm not doing a great job, can you explain to Dr. Jones how this all fits together?*

The majority of Ms. Crutchfield's questions and comments are designed as gentle nudges to her students' learning—affirming that they are on track or helping *them* reflect and notice where adjustment is needed.

IMPLICATIONS?

Preservice teachers: recognize that feedback is absolutely key to student learning. Teaching is not about dispensing knowledge, requiring proof of mastery and then passing judgment on the evidence. It is about *nurturing* learning. Feedback provides the continuous reorientation students need to keep learning in the right direction. You may have to pursue more learning in this area than is required in your education courses. The odds are good that you have delved into the notion of providing feedback to students but have spent less time studying *grading* practices.

Consider the fact that you will probably issue grades of some kind far more often than you implement any particular form of assessment. If grades are such a routine part of your practice, it is well worth your time to study effective grading practices before you default to the practice you have witnessed as a student.

Teachers: here are a few hard words for you. Consider the question posed by long-time grading scholar Tom Guskey: Are you sorting talent or developing talent? Is the effect of your feedback to weed out the "knuckleheads" and elevate and encourage students who are "serious" about their learning? When you speak to students, do your words imply (or even explicitly say) that meeting the demands you make of students—academic and behavioral alike—is a matter of right and wrong? Is your feedback about learning or does it ever venture into judgment?

Please examine your grading practices. Do your practices advance student learning or create barriers to learning (however small or unintentional)? As Rick Wormeli puts it, do the grades you issue function as communication or compensation? Be brave in considering whether the practices you have instituted (in perfectly good faith) are actually doing what they are designed to do and if they are equitable and just.

Administrators: the seat you are in is really hot. The pressure to ensure and increase performance is immense. As we discussed in the previous chapter, keep the focus on learning. Model effective feedback strategies. Articulate the (performance) goal, capture the evidence, provide descriptive feedback *designed to nurture growth*. It is not reasonable to expect teachers to provide effective and appropriate feedback while you model something different.

Faculty: some hard words for you as well. Preservice teachers need to see effective feedback modeled. It is not enough to tell them *about* feedback—even if you do ensure that they explore the concept extensively. Your protégés need to experience effective feedback. Perhaps they have benefited from receiving excellent feedback during their career as a student; they also need to see that practice now from the individuals shaping their conceptions of teaching.

Examine your own grading practices—does your pedagogy in that area model high-quality practice for your students? Make no mistake that nothing undermines the impact of a call to future action as much as the modeling of something very different. Show as much or more than you tell!

WHERE DOES THIS FIT IN TEACHING?

If learning is a cycle, feedback is made up of the actions that bend the process back on itself. The teacher synthesizes his/her knowledge of the students, the subject area, and the best possible practice to form a plan that engages students in relevant, strategically selected learning activities and observes or monitors the students' engagement in those processes and the evidence of the degree to which they are learning. Feedback is the reinvesting of that information into the learning process. Grading and assessment practices that function as endpoints rob students of the opportunity to continue the process of learning.

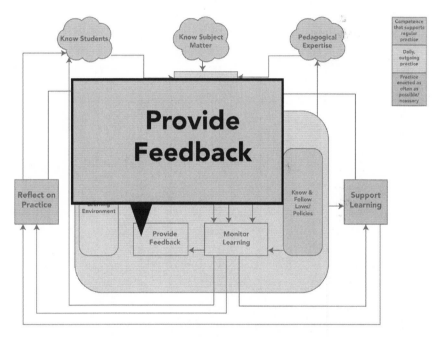

Where Providing Feedback Fits in Teaching. *Source: original digitally created image.*

As with each of the parts of teaching we have explored so far, feedback is itself very complex. There are many ways to provide feedback, many purposes for it, and more than enough opportunity for misunderstanding and ineffective implementation. In the context of this exploration, feedback is yet another area robust enough to support an entire field of study. This complexity within complexity can ironically contribute to the oversimplification of this part and the whole of teaching. After all, to the layman, it is easy to wonder exactly how hard it can be to tell the kids what they got on the test.

Chapter 12

Know and Follow Laws and Policies

An active familiarity and compliance with relevant federal, state, and local laws and policies

The truth is, it is so hard to keep up with all the laws and policies in the teaching world—almost impossible, especially for a new teacher. Knowing them and following them to the best of your abilities, is important. And beyond that, document everything that you attempt to do, knowing that things could fall back on you. (Sarah Waldinger, middle school teacher)

Know and Follow Laws and Policies. *Source: original digitally created image.*

Educational law and policy demand compliance as integral to continued clas-
sification as a teacher in good standing.

Why would "follow the rules" be part of this exploration of what teaching is? This seems odd to include when other practices that are a big part of
teaching (like technology integration) do not have their own sections. These
are fair observations. It is important to recognize this as essential to teaching
because this reality is connected to the larger issue.

As our exploration is demonstrating, teachers are expected to produce
profession-level work. Professionals in other fields are subject to state and
federal laws that apply specifically to that profession—lawyers, architects,
doctors, etc. Education is not unique in this regard but the statutory constraints that teachers face are *professional* requirements and, therefore, are
integral to the nature of teaching itself.

KNOW AND FOLLOW LAWS AND POLICIES

Teaching includes an active familiarity and compliance with relevant federal,
state, and local laws and policies. It is difficult to exaggerate the direct impact
these layers of rules have on teaching. As we will explore later in this chapter,
there are a number of federal statutes that apply directly to teachers or apply
to schools and districts in such a way that they have the effect of impacting
teachers directly. States and local governance entities (such as boards of
education or educational commissions) have the authority to set policy that is
binding on teachers. While these regulations are not often directly contradic-
tory, the cumulative effect generally *is* to place a heavy burden on teachers to
comply, often requiring documentation of that compliance.

WHAT DOES THE RESEARCH SAY?

Although it produced the fewest isolated mentions and (subsequently) codes in
the systematic review of literature that provided the foundation of this exploration of teaching, knowledge of and compliance with laws and policies are an
integral part of teaching practice. Although it may seem irregular to elevate this
issue to the level of other competencies and practices in this study, a simple fact
explains this decision. The professional literature may not focus explicitly on
the importance of knowing and following laws and policies because they are
such an ingrained part of teaching that a special focus would be superfluous.

A great many of the details included in other sections of the study are not
recommendations but required for teachers, either by law or by policy. For
example, one of the ways in which teachers are required to *know students* is

in identifying and addressing the needs of homeless children. In most cases, *knowing their subject matter* is required of teachers by state law; *supporting student learning* is required by federal law. Many schools or districts have policies that make it mandatory for teachers to *monitor* and *provide feedback* on student learning on a regular basis—minimally, in the form of reported numeric and/or A–F grades.

Examples such as these exist throughout the literature. Compliance with educational law and policy certainly is part of job expectations. Indeed, it is this pervasiveness of both law and policy that supports the need for this practice to remain its own category instead of being embedded within others.

Teachers must understand and enact all special education requirements. It is also essential for teachers to comply with required curricula and otherwise follow district- and school-level policies and expectations. These regulations are likely to influence all other areas of professional practice including most or all of the competencies and practices discussed here but also extending into non-instructional duties.

FOR EXAMPLE?

Education law is so complicated that not only does it support its own field of scholarship, it also requires specialization. It is a standard practice for local education agencies (school districts) to rely on legal counsel to review decision-making on a consistent basis. Admittedly, a good portion of the laws and policies that govern public education place constraints on districts, schools, and administrators but even so, many such statutes result in secondary impact on teachers.

To get a glimpse of the place laws and policies play in the work of being a teacher, consider the examples that follow.

Federal laws

- The *Individuals with Disabilities Education Act* requires schools to develop an Individualized Education Plan (IEP) for every student found to meet the guidelines for special education. Teachers are bound by law to be familiar with each student's IEP and to provide the modifications or accommodations articulated in them.
- Section 504 of the 1973 Rehabilitation Act provides rights and service to certain individuals with disabilities. Similar to an IEP, a 504 plan articulates the exact accommodations or modifications that are guaranteed to the student for which it is created. A 504 plan carries the force of law.

- Freedom of speech. While state and federal laws regarding freedom of speech are not designed specifically around schools, they have very serious implications for teachers. Navigating the tension between the right to free speech and the impacts such speech can have can be difficult. Without care, it can be easy to violate a student's rights in the pursuit of all the other priorities a teacher is managing. It can also be difficult to manage the teacher's own right to freedom of expression and how that freedom intersects with other laws and policies.
- Accommodation of religious observances. Federal laws preserving the right of individuals to practice their religion has clear implications for teachers. For example, understanding how issues such as dress code apply to matters of religious expression. Students may be absent from school or parents may object to their child reading specific content on religious grounds. Accommodations of these rights have specific implications for teachers such as developing alternate assignments or redesigning course content or modifying due dates and/or expectations for assignments.
- Other laws that directly impact schools and teachers include Title VI of the Civil Rights Act (which prohibits discrimination on the basis of race, color, and national origin), Title IX (which prohibits discrimination on the bases of sex and requires equal access to co- and extra-curricular activities for female students in particular), Family Educational Rights and Privacy Act (that ensures parents have access to their child's school records and bars any educator from sharing such records with third parties *without the parent's explicit permission*), and other federal statutes and laws.

Every teacher must be familiar with these laws and is bound to comply with them. The impact is significant as teachers must ensure through their planning and practice to remain in compliance with these laws. For example, a teacher seeking to provide students with an authentic learning experience such as investigating a problem in the community and researching possible solutions can find himself on the wrong side of the law if he shares personally identifiable information (name, grade level, etc.) about students with a community organization without parental consent.

Even when actions like these are taken with good intentions and in the attempt to enact a key part of teaching, those intentions will not excuse the violation of federal law.

State laws (a sampling)

- Mandatory reporter. Most states explicitly name teachers as "mandatory reporters." In a nutshell, any teacher (or education employee in some cases) who has reasonable cause to suspect that a student is being abused or neglected *must* report that suspicion to the proper authorities.

- Bullying and harassment. Some states have laws for schools in general and teachers in particular to enforce rules prohibiting bullying and harassment, to report bullying when they observe it, and to facilitate processes that allow students to report bullying not observed by a teacher.
- Cursive writing. Some states have passed laws that mandate very specific action in schools or by teachers. For example, in Alabama, "Lexi's Law" requires that cursive handwriting be taught by the end of third grade.
- Physical restraint. Teachers are required to enforce school and district rules and policies for students. In many states, however, very specific limits are set regarding the actions teachers are allowed to take to do so. For example, in some places, teachers are not permitted to physically restrain a student (even if the student is engaged in dangerous or violent behavior) unless the teacher has received formal training on how to apply physical restraint safely.
- Administration of medicine. In most states, teachers are not allowed to provide students with medication of any kind for any reason unless they have "medication training" and are authorized to dispense specific medications to a student. Giving aspirin to a student with a headache is unlawful in many places.
- Ethical behavior. Teachers are included in state ethics laws. These stipulate ranges of behaviors that are deemed ethical and unethical. For example, it is unethical for teachers to use any school property for personal matters. Some states have laws stipulating that educators may not accept gifts from students or parents unless they are of "de minimis" (trivial) value.
- Collecting money. Although this exploration explicitly acknowledges and sets aside the tasks and expectations that are part of the job of a teacher but are not *teaching*, many of those extraneous (but generally required) tasks are well regulated—as demonstrated in the current list already. Among actions that a teacher might be required to take for any variety of reasons is the collection of money from students, parents, or other parties for official purposes. The law and local regulations very tightly control exactly how this process must be conducted. The handling of funds can be a significant stressor for teachers as mismanagement (even unintentional) can carry severe penalties, including termination of employment.

Most states have *dozens* of laws that apply to teachers either directly or indirectly. Some states have laws designed to protect and preserve the rights of teachers themselves; all have laws designed to protect students; most have laws that aim to guarantee outcomes or results for students. In all cases, remaining aware of and compliant with all state laws is the responsibility of the individual. That burden frequently includes a requirement for schools to formally notify all employees of the applicable law(s) each year.

Local policy (examples)

- Curriculum and resources. School districts are explicitly authorized to make decisions regarding the details of the purchasing and implementation of instructional resources and the local curriculum. In effect, a district has a great deal of leeway in what it requires of teachers in terms of what is taught and how it is taught. This can include requiring a specific instructional product or program, implementing specific instructional strategies, or incorporating any number of instructional actions as part of the district's curriculum.
- Schedules. Districts and schools set the school-year calendar and the master schedule for schools. These decisions have a direct effect on teachers and their practice. For example, some secondary schools run "block" schedules that feature class periods that are up to 90 minutes long; others run schedules that include six, seven, or eight periods each day that last as little as 40 minutes. Schools or districts sometimes also stipulate at least some of the details of an elementary teacher's schedule—requiring an uninterrupted block of instructional time for reading, limiting or eliminating recess times, and assigning guidelines or specific times for art, music, physical education, library visits and other parts of the day outside the "homeroom."
- Dress code. Most school districts have a dress code for employees. While the language and details vary, they are mostly variations of "dress 'professionally' when you are at work."
- Social media usage. Some school districts have policies governing employees' use of social media, even outside work hours. This is an area where freedom of speech protections and "ethical behavior" standards intersect. Schools and districts usually *can* impose some level of control over a teacher's social media activity.
- Ethical behavior. Most school districts enact policies explicitly prohibiting a range of unethical or inappropriate behavior. Some such policies may seem unnecessary or redundant to state or federal laws but are codified at the local level either as required by state law or as a way of doubly ensuring the expectation is clear—the prohibition of harassment, of theft, of maintaining inappropriate relationships with students, of using one's position for personal gain, and many others.

School and district administrators are generally held responsible for informing teachers and other school employees of the laws and policies that apply to them. The responsibility for complying with them, however, ultimately falls to the individual.

IMPLICATIONS?

Policy-makers: this observation should not be read as a criticism of the making of laws and policies that apply to teachers. Instead, consider the fact of the great number of policies and statutes that constrain teachers to act in specific ways. Recognize that a vocation important enough to necessitate this amount of oversight should be treated as a profession. A profession owed the rights and privileges demanded by and granted to other professions.

Do not neglect your duty to provide oversight to teaching. But as you do, consider whether the laws and policies you create and enforce are designed to regulate highly skilled professionals or to control laborers, essential though they may be.

Administrators: attend to the proportionality of your interactions with teachers. There is no doubt that the leadership and supervision of any group of humans is messy. We are fallible creatures. A question to hold in the forefront of your mind is whether the manner in which you address *any* issue, concern, or deficiency is in proportion to the problem within the framework of the complexity of teaching.

To be clear, this admonition does not apply to felonious or grossly unethical activity. On the other hand, there are dozens of ways to run afoul of policy completely unintentionally and even in the pursuit of other mandates. When it is necessary for you to enforce policy (and it often is), consider the way in which you go about that work. In this very complex, very difficult profession if you position yourself as a righteous enforcer of the rules, policies, and laws *as more important than the professionals they are designed around*, expect to see negative impact to your organization's culture and to your ability to lead effectively.

Teachers: you already know that education is highly regulated and that your state legislature and your school board are more likely to create new regulations than not every year. You may not even think of knowing and complying with laws and polices as part of *teaching* itself. It *is* though, particularly when a specific part of the work you do can be explicitly mandated by law at any time or something new added with the same burden of compliance.

In addition to the expectation that school and district administrators keep you informed of changes to laws and policies, you should take steps to stay tuned to and understand such details. If you have not read your district's policy manual, you should. If you do not read the minutes of your school board's minutes, you should. Yes, others should keep you informed. But as a professional, you should also ensure for yourself that you know the rules, policies, and laws that govern your work.

Preservice teachers: don't panic! You need to know federal law and have very likely studied the key laws already. If you know what state you will be working in, it would be worth your time to seek a basic familiarity with educational law specific to that state. In most cases, it will make sense to delve into local district policies at the time you are hired. Your peers and supervisors *will* help you learn the details. The rules and policies are sincerely not designed to trap or trip teachers; minor mistakes made in good faith are forgivable. As with other areas, the take-away should not be fear but awareness of the complexity of the job and what is expected of you.

WHERE DOES THIS FIT IN TEACHING?

If you were to ask one hundred teachers to list everything that is part of the act and process of teaching (not necessarily the entire job), it seems likely that fewer than ten would mention anything about the laws and policies that govern teaching directly. But, as we explored briefly in this chapter, nearly every part of teaching is impacted by either a state or federal law or by a local policy. The role these regulations play in the act and process of teaching goes beyond the influence of laws on the actions of workers in general; education law is both vast and specific to the profession and to the professionals doing the work.

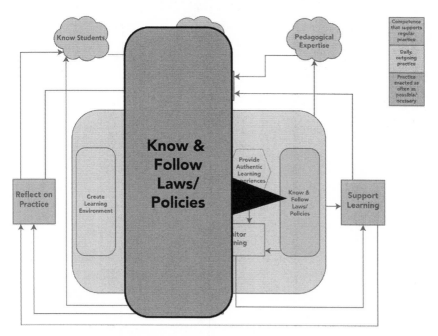

Where the Knowledge and Following of Laws and Policies Fits in Teaching. *Source: original digitally created image.*

There can be no argument that knowledge of and compliance with these statutes is optional; this *is* an essential part of teaching. We recognize it as its own part of teaching because teaching requires a continuous accounting for and complying with regulations. The way a teacher supports learning is directly impacted by students' IEPs and 504 plans. The content of a lesson is directly impacted by the district's curriculum and the specific requirements it includes. The strategies the teacher selects for tomorrow's lesson are heavily influenced by the list of strategies the school has articulated as a required part of practice.

Chapter 13

Reflect on Practice

A continuous, deep reflection on professional practice for the purpose of improvement

Teaching is a way of life. You've got to plan, you've got to know your students, you've got to go home and think about what worked, what didn't work. It's not an eight to three job. It's not from end of August to May, you know. It's all through the summer. You're still planning, you're still thinking whether you might be going to workshops or conferences or thinking of how to arrange your classroom next year. You know, I mean, it's a constant. Teaching is a whole big huge gray area. There's no yes or no, right or wrong. There's a lot of what ifs.
(Brandi Morris, elementary teacher)

Reflect on Practice

Reflection on Practice. *Source: original digitally created image.*

Reflection is integral to effective teaching and essential to continued professional growth.

Reflection is a practice so deeply embedded within teaching that many teachers might not think to name it as a separate, essential part of the job. To teach effectively, however, requires constant monitoring of all the available evidence and data to drive the dozens—and often hundreds—of decisions that a teacher must make every day.

Given the complexity and the demanding nature of teaching, it can be tempting to take the actions planned for a particular lesson or day of school and move on. But accomplished teachers develop the habit both of fast, continuous reflective analysis of the evidence they see as lessons unfold and of systematic, thoughtful reflection on the efficacy of strategies and actions after the action is over.

REFLECT ON PRACTICE

Because teaching is so complex, it is essential for teachers to develop the habit of engaging in reflection frequently in order to guide both immediate and future decisions.

It is reasonable to notice that while reflection is often a point of emphasis in teacher education programs, it is a discipline that is too easily omitted from a teacher's practice. Reflection may not be perceived as an integral part of teaching by some teachers because it is not part of their practice. Schools and districts are more likely to explicitly expect teachers to engage in most of the other aspects of teaching but only *encourage* reflection—if it is made a point of emphasis at all.

Reflection is, however, *embedded* in many practices that schools and districts prioritize. For example, "professional learning communities" is one framework for undertaking collective planning for instruction. This framework is built around core questions for teams of teachers to consider. These questions are designed to elicit *reflective* analysis from the teachers individually and collectively. Questions like "How will we respond when some students do not learn?" are intended to spark thought and consideration by the team.

Whether or not schools promote specific structures to encourage teachers to be reflective in their work, it is clear that it is essential to effective teaching.

WHAT DOES THE RESEARCH SAY?

Effective teachers reflect on their teaching, engaging in an ongoing process of self-reflection and analysis. This practice is enabled by an examination of the actions, decisions, and consequences that shape him/her and an awareness of his/her own positionality and identity development.

This process of identifying and examining one's own positionality is particularly important given that many teachers serve students whose own backgrounds and positionality is likely to be very different from that of the teacher. Unexamined, these differences can be the cause of ineffective teaching and learning cycles. While differences are not inherently problematic, failure to recognize and account for them can be.

Building on this self-awareness, the effective teacher actively analyzes lesson plans, student responses and activities during lessons, and student work samples; observes videos of his/her own teaching; collaborates closely with peers in examining evidence of student learning overall; and makes purposeful use of all such reflections to improve practice. Reflection serves as a mechanism for testing the efficacy of practice and maintaining, improving, or replacing it based on the evidence.

Teaching is by its nature developmental; teachers who engage in deeply reflective practice tend to develop professional expertise more rapidly. Beyond immediate changes to practice, the reflective process drives the setting and monitoring of professional goals and striving to improve professional efficacy.

FOR EXAMPLE?

There is no list of "right" reflection questions. There *are* plenty of suggestions out there of reflection questions a teacher can ask. Notice that questions that evoke reflection effectively have a few things in common.

- Evidence-based. Reflection is about identifying the facts and considering them through a critical lens.
- Analysis. Great reflection questions demand sense-making.
- Conclusions. The point of reflection is not the noticing; it is noticing *in order to make decisions* about what happens next.

There may be additional characteristics but these represent the essence of great reflection questions. Note that it can take a *series* of questions to get to the reflection.

Any blog or article or book (including this one) that purports to provide *the* list on anything should be reviewed with a grain of salt—openness to the value of the details included mixed with skepticism that perfection has been captured. Given that caveat, it may be helpful to consider a few reflection questions recommended by a variety of teachers, authors, and organizations. The following is meant to illustrate how reflective questions are constructed, not as a recommended list for use.

- Did the goals of this lesson connect to the unit of study? Did student's learning today connect to or extend their learning from yesterday?
- To what extent did I achieve the lesson's goals? What evidence do I have to support this conclusion?
- Did the instructional strategies I chose for the lesson today help the students meet the learning target? How do I know?
- What challenges are inherent in teaching the ideas or skills included in today's learning target? How did I account for those challenges in my planning?
- Did I deviate from my lesson plan? Why? Did that deviation help or slow learning? How do I know?
- Did (all) students have choices in my class today? What type of choices? What effect did choice have on students' learning?
- What opportunity(ies) did I miss today?
- Did this lesson have value for students who had mastered the learning target before it even started? In what way?
- What characteristics of these student work samples demonstrate partial or full mastery of the learning target?
- How did my feedback to students promote growth toward the learning target?
- Is the content of my grade book an accurate reflection of student learning?
- What did I learn about individual students today that I can incorporate into tomorrow's lesson to their advantage?
- Are the relationships I have with students helping or hurting their ability to learn?
- If I teach this lesson again, what should I do differently?
- What do I need to learn next? Do I know where/how to learn that thing?
- What are the biggest obstacles to improving my practice? What can I do to overcome them?

According to John Dewey, "we do not learn from experience. We learn from reflecting on experience." It is this part of teaching that allows us to convert experience into expertise. By learning from every mistake and capturing the *reason* for every success, the process of reflection can turn both into the material for constructing future success.

IMPLICATIONS?

Preservice teachers: trust your professors. Those reflection exercises they make you do *are* critical to becoming an effective teacher. Think of them as practice; reflection is not a task but a habit—it does not work as well if it is always done under duress. Dedicate yourself willingly, then, to the opportunity to begin developing a habit that will serve you well as a teacher.

Faculty: you probably know that writing reflections are not your students' favorite activity. Do not waver on developing that discipline. Consider a variety of reflective exercises: written, personal reflections on a lesson or observation; group review of facts and evidence for reflection (modeled after a PLC meeting, for example); think-alouds to model your own reflection on teaching and learning as it is happening.

In addition to equipping future teachers with the skills to survive the steep learning curve of the job, also plant the seeds of habits that will propel them toward continuous growth and learning as a result of their reflexive reflection on *everything*.

Teachers: if you have read this far you know that the thesis of this book is that teaching is impossibly complex and difficult. You might be tempted to beg off this part of teaching. It is time-consuming and it is often challenging to one's ego. "What could be better" can feel a *lot* like "what did I do wrong." Have the courage to ask yourself questions when you don't feel like it. Make the space to pursue incremental growth. "One and done" professional learning sessions (probably the majority of what you experience) cannot affect meaningful growth.

It is a commitment to getting just a little bit better each day that will yield growth that is sustainable and far more impactful in the long run. Your own candid reflection on your practice is the strongest possible driver of that process.

Administrators: two challenges for you. First, stop the "PD for all" model. Quit cold turkey. Right now. Respect to you if you already have; you are uncommon. Spraying everyone with a professional learning session or series is *much* easier to arrange, manage, and monitor. But you *must* know that differentiation applies to all learners, not just K–12 students. Teachers as (professional) learners need differentiated learning opportunities. And, just like their students, teachers need a voice in that process.

The companion challenge is to build a culture of intentional reflection. Instead of rolling through with an observation checklist, ask teachers one thought-provoking question to ponder (and to keep the answer to themselves). In other words, *model* the process of reflection by building a culture of reflection. Strong schools require strong teachers. Your part is to nurture the professional practices that incubate growth. High on that list is purposeful reflection.

WHERE DOES THIS FIT IN TEACHING?

If feedback is the part of teaching that bends the process back on itself, reflection is the part that turns experience into expertise. Reflection allows the teacher to capitalize on his/her experiences and parlay them into professional growth. It is entirely possible—and unfortunately common—to fail to learn from experience. Without habitual reflection, a teacher will still develop professional habits. He/she will get better at completing specific tasks and more adept at parts of teaching over time. But reflection is a great accelerant of learning. It makes both success and struggle valuable to learning. It is an indispensable part of accomplished teaching.

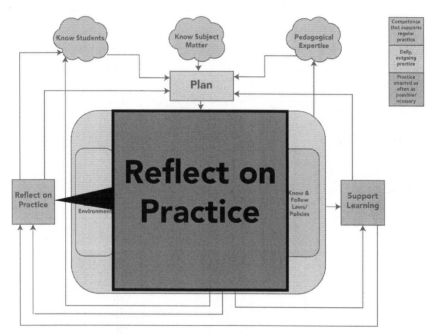

Where Reflection Fits in Teaching. *Source: original digitally created image.*

If you're not reflecting to figure out what's going on and what's happening and how to move past it, then you're not trying to learn yourself (Ronald Passmore, high school CTE teacher).

Chapter 14

What Does It All Mean?

*The bell keeps ringing, metaphorically and every time the bell rings you have to
be all of those things. That's on your job description every single day—to mani-
fest the fullness of teaching. Because that one day that you're not that thing,
that's the very day that you will get observed, that's the very day that a parent
will have a gripe, that's the very day that you'll beat yourself up because you
weren't all things to all people because you were so busy being other things.
That's the complexity of teaching that everyone needs to understand, that teachers are called upon to be every check in the box every time the bell rings. And
the very moment that you're not all those things, that may be the time that you
live to regret.* (Dr. Lisa Stewart, high school teacher)

Here at the end of our tour of teaching—as described by the research literature and affirmed by teachers—let us reflect briefly on what we have seen
and what it might mean. Once again, the act and process of teaching includes
thirteen competencies and practices. These are not practices that may enhance
teaching or ideas for the maximization of teaching; they *are* teaching.

This is not to argue that every individual employed as a teacher in fact
demonstrates each of these competencies or engages in all of these practices.
This is not to claim that everyone who is a teacher agrees that these *should* all
be part of teaching. No profession could claim that every person in its ranks
faithfully discharges even the duties and tasks explicitly required of the job.
Examples of teaching that do not include parts of this description do not disprove the case for the complexity of teaching. Instead, they serve as evidence
that teaching is so overwhelmingly complex as it exists in the abstract that it
is almost literally impossible to fully enact in reality.

We began this exploration with the metaphor of a guided tour. As this tour ends, let us review the pieces of teaching that we have noticed: the thirteen competencies and practices.

- Know students. Knowing individual students deeply in a range of dimensions and using that knowledge to drive professional decisions.
- Know the subject matter. Holding, demonstrating, and expanding strong content knowledge.
- Demonstrate pedagogical expertise. Understanding and enacting effective professional practices related to instruction.
- Plan for practice. Routine, strategic, thoughtful planning for both short- and long-term actions.
- Create a learning environment. Strategic, continuous action to create and maintain an environment optimally conducive to learning.
- Engage students in learning. Implementation of activities designed to actively engage students in learning.
- Implement effective strategies. Knowing which specific instructional strategies work well to support learning and enacting them.
- Provide authentic learning experiences. Designing and implementing learning activities that are meaningful and relevant to students.
- Support learning. Identifying and providing a wide range of supports to advance student learning.
- Monitor learning. Actively and continuously monitoring the degree to which students are learning.
- Provide feedback. Continuously providing specific, descriptive, individual feedback to students about their learning.
- Know and follow laws and policies. An active familiarity and compliance with relevant federal, state, and local laws and policies.
- Reflect on practice. A continuous, deep reflection on professional practice for the purpose of improvement.

As you look at this map, notice two key things. First, each one of these competencies and practices has great depth and complexity of its own. Every one of them is nuanced enough to support an entire body of research, to sustain an ecosphere of professional learning materials and experiences, and (in most cases) to support the building of entire careers in the study and exposition of that single area. *Each part* of teaching requires a significant effort to reach something reasonably considered competence, let alone masterful practice.

Second, no part of these competencies and practices exists in a vacuum. For the purpose of this exploration we have examined them individually but it would be foolish to expect to see clear lines of demarcation around any one of them in practice. That fact underscores the idea that the omission of even one part of this whole will—at the least—be accompanied by a weakness in practice in other areas.

For example, a teacher who makes little effort to know students will struggle to plan effectively because he is planning for hypothetical students, not his actual students. A teacher who is unskilled in monitoring student learning will struggle to provide feedback that is meaningful to their learning. A teacher who has not created a healthy learning environment will struggle to engage her students in deep and meaningful learning. The component parts of teaching are distinct but tightly intertwined.

There is one additional essential observation we must make in the context of exploring the nature of teaching. This exploration has been limited to the *act and process* of teaching. It is crucial to recognize that there is a significant list of tasks, duties, and responsibilities that teachers *must* discharge as a matter of course that do not fall within the boundaries of the act and process of teaching itself.

These include supervision tasks (bus, hall, lunchroom duty); planning, organizing, and conducting extra-curricular events (dances, clubs, etc.); paperwork, communication, planning and logistics required to conduct co-curricular events (fieldtrips, academic competitions, etc.); fundraising and the collection of money for all manner of reasons and events; all the clerical tasks adjacent to or even wholly outside parts of the act and process of teaching; and many more. We have explored the complexity of teaching, not even the full complexity of what it means *to be a teacher*. Recognize as fact that however complex *teaching* is, being a teacher is always more complex.

IMPLICATIONS

Remember, this book is a map. It is designed as an exploration of teaching. But sometimes, maps also include observations that can suggest action. So in that spirit, consider a handful of possible implications for just a few groups of individuals to whom this exploration most directly applies.

Teachers: first and most importantly, do not accept this book as a criticism of your practice and resist any efforts of others to use it that way. This book does not argue that teaching *should* be complex and all teachers *should* meet all of these expectations; it points out that teaching *is* complex and that such complexity implies systematic actions and approaches that are missing. Do consider a few reflection questions.

- Does this description of teaching fit with my experience of teaching?
- What essential parts of teaching (the act and process, not the whole job) as I experience it are missing from this description?

- Does this shine a flashlight on any area I have not nurtured much in my practice?
- Given the complexity of teaching, what could I do *next* to grow my expertise?
- How can I use this description of the complexity of teaching to help advocate for the profession?

Administrators: consider this a call to action. It seems reasonable to predict that the profession is in danger of literally running out of teachers *and* that fully reversing that trend will require systemic solutions. But individual administrators can take immediate action. Your actions can matter. Consider a few reflection questions.

- Do I recognize in this exploration an accurate representation of teaching? Is teaching really this complex?
- Does my work as a leader acknowledge that teaching is complex or is that complexity the elephant we all see but never acknowledge? Do I ever think of teacher concerns and advocacy as complaining?
- Do I affirm the work of teachers pursuing excellence in the complexity? When I do, does that sound like specific, descriptive feedback or do I tend to offer the general "Thanks for *all you do*"?
- Do I consider each of my decisions through the lens of the complexity of teaching? Would any of my decisions be different if I did?
- Is my work currently contributing to the professionalization of teaching or am I (even unintentionally) helping to de-professionalize teaching?
- What role should I play in advocating for public education in general and the teaching profession in particular?

Preservice teachers: this is the profession you have chosen. This discussion of the complexity of teaching is not intended to surprise or frighten you. But it is right for you to have a clear picture of the scope of the profession you are entering. The work is difficult both because of its volume and because much of it requires studied expertise.

Hopefully you have learned from teachers who have modeled excellence in each of these areas of practice. Most teachers are driven by a great passion for their students; you have likely witnessed that passion and heard them talk about their dedication to their students. It is equally unlikely that you have heard your teachers talk about themselves as professionals.

Accept here a challenge to create and hold a mental image of yourself as a *professional* educator. You are asked to dedicate yourself to the mastery and enactment of professional work. Your future students expect that from you. You, in turn, should expect the rights and privileges owed to a professional. You are not "just a teacher"; you are an educator!

Carry a few questions with you as you continue on your journey to become an accomplished teacher.

- What one thing will I do today to hone my craft as a teacher?
- As I gain experience and grow as a professional, what next learning focus for *me* would have the greatest benefit to my students' learning?
- Which group(s) of teachers am I part of that facilitate and accelerate my learning? Where can I find a group to help me pursue the learning I am focused on now?
- How will I conduct myself in order to defy the label of "just a teacher"? How will I respond when that messaging comes at me either explicitly or implicitly embedded in structures and traditions in education and the society at large?

Faculty: you already know the critical role you play in public education. You must recognize that you are not immune from the existential threat public education faces; this issue concerns you as much as it concerns your students. One of the purposes of this text is to trace the complexity of teaching plays in order to consider the role that complexity might play in the de-professionalization of teaching, particularly when that complexity is not recognized and honored as such. As both a scholar and a teacher yourself, consider a few questions to ponder.

- Does my program and do my own courses show preservice teachers the complexity of teaching? Are we cherry-picking a few trees to examine or do we give our students at least a sense of the whole forest?
- Do preservice teachers leave my class/program with foundational knowledge in these thirteen competencies and practices? What exactly do I do to nurture growth in each area?
- When preservice teachers finish my program, do they have the habits of mind to continue developing their expertise as professional educators?
- How well do I model these thirteen competencies and practices? Do preservice teachers learn the *theory* of teaching from me or do they also see it modeled?
- In what way(s) could my scholarship contribute to the professionalization of teaching?

Parents: if you are reading this book, you are deeply invested in education. Thank you for that support. While the majority of this book has not been addressed to you directly, you are a key audience for the implications that rise from noticing the great complexity of teaching. If you have been disappointed by your experiences with the educational system, do not give into the temptation to weaponize this description of teaching. Substandard practice *does* exist in education but there is no lack of identifying and sanctioning weakness.

You should be a strong advocate for excellence locally. You should expect much from teachers. That expectation is far more likely to yield powerful results when it is accompanied with localized efforts to elevate the profession—to treat teachers like professionals: high expectations paired with the dignity, status, voice, and privileges afforded other accomplished professionals.

Perhaps these questions may be helpful in digesting what you have read here.

- In what ways does this influence my understanding of the nature of teaching?
- Is this what teaching looks like in my community?
- What do teachers and schools need to make teaching look like this? What can I do to help ensure they have what they need?
- What can I do to help make the schools in my community a place where accomplished teachers want to work?

Decision-makers: the very best outcome of this exploration of teaching is a positive impact on your thinking. Whether you are a local or state board member, a state or national legislator, or an influencer of policy, you are the most important audience of this work. You have the most authority and influence to act on the implications here.

Here is the very simple heart of the matter: teaching is massively complex but teachers are consistently *not* treated like professionals. **That** is the elephant we just refuse to talk about. That mismatch (between the demands and the benefits of the profession) is a major driver of the undeniable shortage of teachers we face today.

The case for what to do with this fact has already been made by others: professionalize teaching. Radically. Fully. Swiftly.

While the work of professionalizing teaching cannot be done by any single hand, it is well worth your while to consider what role you can play in advancing that work. You can use one or more of the following questions to prompt your thinking.

Can I *see* a mismatch? If we demand profession-level work from teachers, do we treat them like professionals in my district/area/state?

Is there a connection between the evaporating teacher talent pool and the complexity of teaching as it really exists around here?

What decisions have I made, what policies have I enacted, what actions have I taken that has made teaching more complex? Setting aside the importance of any one of them, are the demands we make of teachers reasonable when taken together?

Do I believe that we could reverse the talent drain from teaching if we worked to truly professionalize it? If so, what would it take to do that? Am I willing to help take those steps? Where should I start?

How different would my decision-making about education be if I paused to remember this complexity every time before I made a decision?

EXIT SLIP

As every accomplished teacher knows, the very end of class presents an opportunity to lock in learning. When planned well, simple activities designed to underscore and preserve learning can be powerful.

If you are still here at the end of this tour, ponder just one more question as you go: if I can see this elephant in the classroom, what then ought I to do?

About the Author

Andrew Maxey has been a public school educator since his teaching career began in 1999. Since then, he has been a high school Language Arts teacher in rural Indiana, San Diego, and Alabama. He has been a building-level administrator at the elementary, middle, and high school levels and has held a variety of district-level administrative positions.

Andrew is frankly a little obsessed with what he views as critical issues in education: effective assessment and grading practices, middle-level practice actually informed by a deep knowledge of young adolescence and educational leadership. He has become especially vocal about the complexity of teaching and the ongoing deprofessionalization of teaching in the last few years. As Director of Strategic Initiatives in Tuscaloosa, Alabama, he seeks to align all his work with the empowerment and uplift of teachers—which he considers the best hope for serving students in any meaningful way. He considers it his moral obligation to ask questions, take risks, and protect/advocate for those in his sphere of influence.

As the father of three girls, who have started a collective eleven-year passage through their teen years (at the time of publication), he is doubly committed to advocating for the professionalization of teaching; for the sake of *their* children.